# The Bungalow

# THE BUNGALOW

### America's Arts and Crafts Home

## PAUL DUCHSCHERER
## PHOTOGRAPHS BY DOUGLAS KEISTER

**PENGUIN STUDIO**

(*Overleaf*) Front porch of a bungalow in Pasadena, California. Extending a warm welcome, Lori King and David Heller's front porch provides the informal transition from outdoors to indoors that characterizes many bungalows. Because it serves as an outdoor living room, it handily expands the capacity of its counterpart just inside. The original 1911 front door at the right, with its Craftsman-style detailing rendered in quarter-sawn oak and beveled-glass panels, is similar to many variations found in bungalow-plan books of the period. A vintage wicker porch swing and chair provide a favorite spot for relaxing beneath a suspended art-glass panel. Adjustable bamboo blinds also contribute a cozy sense of enclosure to the space, while admitting softly filtered sunlight and garden views.

PENGUIN STUDIO
Published by the Penguin Group
Penguin Books USA Inc., 375 Hudson Street,
New York, New York, 10014, U.S.A.

Penguin Books Ltd, 27 Wrights Lane,
London W8 5TZ, England

Penguin Books Australia Ltd, Ringwood,
Victoria, Australia

Penguin Books Canada Ltd, 2801 John Street,
Markham, Ontario, Canada L3R 1B4

Penguin Books (N.Z.) Ltd, 182-90 Wairau Road,
Auckland 10, New Zealand

Penguin Books Ltd, Registered Offices:
Harmondsworth, Middlesex, England

First published by Penguin Studio, an imprint of Penguin Books USA Inc.

First printing, November 1995
10 9 8 7 6

Library of Congress Catalog Card Number: 95-60165

Book designed by Marilyn Rey
Printed and bound by Dai Nippon Printing Co., Hong Kong, Ltd.

ISBN: 0-670-86353-X

This book is dedicated to the recognition
and preservation of America's bungalows,
and to all the people who have
recognized and preserved them.

# ACKNOWLEDGMENTS

Tracking down and photographing the houses for this book was an enormous task. Thankfully, many people helped us along the way. First and foremost were the owners and occupants of the bungalows that appear in this book. Their commitment to preserving this important part of America's architectural heritage and their hard work are to be applauded. The homeowners and/or occupants include the following persons: John Abbott, David and Jackie Allswang, Frances Arnold, Russ Attwater, Michael and Glenna Barrett, Pearl Beach and Steve Johnson, Mike Besoli, Judith Bond, Edward Bosley and staff at the Gamble House, John Brinkman, Jill Gannon and George Murray, at *American Bungalow* magazine, Kay and Bob Cheatham, Marleen Deane, Dr. and Mrs. Dixon, David and Stephanie Edens, Victoria Eisen and David Wampler, Ferris, Johnson & Perkins Architects, Inc., Lawrence Finkel and Anna Penna, Gary and Evelyn Glenn, Scott and Lauren Goldstein, John Gouveia, Ray Grieshaber, John Gussman, Timothy Heney, Judy and Lee Hilburg, Rod Holcomb and Jane Brackman, Melinda Chase Holt, Marilyn Hulbert and Kip Fout, Mr. and Mrs. George D. Jagels, Jr., Paul Johnson, Ted Ketos, Cindy King, Lori King and David Heller/Arroyo Style, Allan and Deborah Kropp, Tom and Traci Lech, Virginia and Quentin Lish, Gary and Jamie Little, Paul Little, Caro Macpherson, Bob and Paula Marshall, Sam and Mary Martinez, Scott and Betsy Mathieson, Robert and Marie McConnell, Lynne McDaniel, Jim and Paula McHargue, Mike and Linda McNally, Pam-Anela Messenger and Howard Martin, Carol Michel, Ken Miedema and Julie Reiz, David and Kim Minichiello, John Mitchell, Monty Montgomery, Cate Muther and Dennis Aftergut, John Oster, Melissa Patton, Edward and Mary Phillips, Gussie and Isom Porter, Vasti Porter, Roger Pritchard, Marilyn Raack and Jim Bixler, David Raposa and Ed Trosper, Bob and Dolores Rhoads, Brad and Daisy Roe, Randy Sappenfield, Tom and Toni Sestak, Margie Shapiro and Ian Hinchcliffe, John Shimek, Peggy Page Smith, David Swarens and Vykki Mende Gray, Charles and Juliet Sykes, Leslie Thornley, Angela Tonielli, Helen Wadman, Connie and Mike Whalen, Michael Wheelden, Dr. Robert Winter, and Mark Yerko.

Unfortunately, space limitations meant that we could not include all of the bungalows that we wished. Those dedicated homeowners whose homes we photographed but could not include in the body of the book are: Earl Alderman, Richard Barbeau, Mrs. P.M. Barceloux, Linda Boyd and Mathew Smith, John Carroll and Tracy Johnston, Pat Colombe, Paul Crane, Steve and Liz Doubleday, Gerald Edwards, Mr. and Mrs. George Enos, Alice Erber and Rob Steinberg, Glenn Faulk, James and Martha Franchi, Ron Hartsough, Jenny Jenkins, Richard and Shelly Jose, Lois I. Kloss, Jane Lande, M.S. Levy, Mathew Lifschiz, Diane Lindquist, Theresa Liu, Terry Matoba, Terry Meng and Peter Dreier, B.J. Miller, Matt Murphy, Charles Nolan, Robert and Pat Rayburn, Penny & John Sherry, Norman and Martha Sollid, Helen Stauer, Nancy Stewart, Erik Walberg and Judith Wells-Walberg, Laurel White, and Larry Word and Don Bean.

Special thanks go to all those who helped us along the way. Many supplied leads and information and their expert guidance turned what could have been an ordeal into an adventure. Thanks to Alameda Victorian Preservation Society, City of Alameda Historical Advisory Board, Judith Altschuler, Rob Anderson, Artistic License of San Francisco, V. Michael Ashford, Molly and Steve Attell, Dianne Ayres and Timothy Hansen/Arts & Crafts Period Textiles, Nancy Baer, Joan and Robert Banning, Mitchell Barnhart and Amando Sierras, Berkeley Architectural Heritage Association, Judy Benda, Nina Bookbinder, Bruce Bradbury, Peter Bridgman, Andrea Brown, Bungalow Heaven Landmark District, Chris Buntmeyr, John Burrows/J.R. Burrows & Co., Charlene Casey, Scott Cazet, Odell Childress and Don Weggeman, Susan Christman, Sheila Cook, Don and Karen Covington, James and Geraldine Duchscherer, Kenneth Duchscherer, Steven Duchscherer and Sandy Wynn, Hank Dunlop, Mr. and Mrs. Gerald Edwards, John Fellows, Susan Fennimore, Amy Forbes, Carolyn S. Gaiennie, Joe Garcia, Bennye Gatteys and Richard Bail, Cheryl Gordon, Ora Gosey, Vicki Granowitz, Daniel Gregory/*Sunset* magazine, Erik Hanson and Ingrid Helton, Jill Harris, Kay Haugaad, Sady Hayashita Architects, Timothy Holton, Bruce Hutchison, Suzie Hyder, David Kahn, Katherine Keister, Michael and Jeanne Khanchalian, Peggy King, Robert Kneisel, Erik Kramvik, John Kurtz, Michael Larsen and Elizabeth Pomada/Literary Agents, Norman Larson, Jeanne and Mark Lazzarini, Jack Leutza, Mark and Abby Lew, Suzy Locke, Margaret Maclean, Barney Marinelli, Jeff Marx, Wayne Mathes, Jan McHargue, Woodruff C. Minor, Monrovia Old House Preservation Group, Joni Monnich, David Nunley, Louise Padden and Evert Brown, Pasadena Heritage, Patricia Poore and Kate Gatchell at Dovetale Publishers, Peter Post, Debra Richards, Stephen Rynerson and Pat O'Brien/Rynerson-O'Brien Architecture, Ann Sansberry, Ken Sarna and the production staff at Bradbury & Bradbury Art Wallpapers, Phil and Nancy Skonieczki, Robert Sedlock, Jr., Sussman & Associates, Pat Suzuki, Lennox Tierney, Therese Tierney, Robert and Kelly Tatosian/Arroyo Craftsman Lighting, Doni Tunheim, Victorian Preservation Association/San Jose, Ed Pinson and Debra Ware, West Adams Heritage Association, Martin Eli Weil, Roger Williams, Kurt and Jennifer Wilson, Paul and Nina Winans/Winans Construction, Diana Woodbridge, Gary Yuschalk and Larkin Mayo/Victorian Interiors, and Debey Zito.

Lastly, we want to single out some very special people. Sandy Schweitzer, John Freed, and Don Merrill encouraged us with their words and their labor, and our intrepid editor extraordinaire, Cyril Nelson, was always there to lend his expert advice and guidance.

The search goes on to find candidates for a bungalow book with a national scope. Please send snapshots and information about worthy bungalows in your area to Douglas Keister, 5826 Fremont Street, Oakland, California 94608.

# CONTENTS

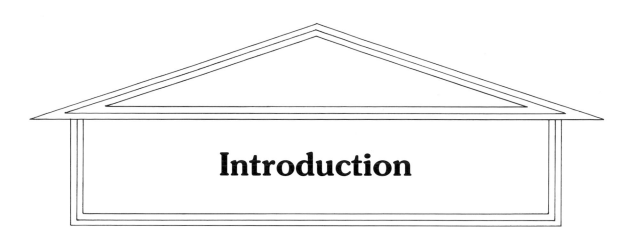

# Introduction

## Defining the Bungalow

### ITS ORIGINS AND EVOLUTION

What exactly is a bungalow? One definition is as close as the nearest dictionary: "A dwelling of a type first developed in India, usually one story, with low sweeping lines and a wide verandah."[1] Another dictionary states: "1. A small cottage, usually of one story. 2. In India, a thatched or tiled house having one story and surrounded by a wide verandah."[2] These definitions sound simple and straightforward enough, until an attempt is made to apply them to the bungalow as it has come to be known in America. Then, the confusion over exactly how "physically" to define the bungalow, or even what may be technically called one, is due to the various and sometimes conflicting ways the term has been used and documented in our culture over many years. It seems that when things fall into the realm of popular culture as the bungalow did, conversational liberties are taken in a casual or even humorous reference, compounding the problem of its true definition. One such remark, documented in Henry H. Saylor's popular book *Bungalows* first published in 1911, offered the facetious suggestion "that in the new dictionaries a bungalow should be defined as a house that looks as if it had been built for less money than it actually cost" (which brings up another subject entirely).

In any case, few standard reference works such as dictionaries or encyclopedias have attempted to delve into the matter in any depth, and clearly the information usually supplied is inconclusive, or noncommittal at best. For example, even in the first of the dictionary definitions quoted here, there is room for interpretation in the phrase "usually one story," which seems to suggest that there might be some unusual bungalows of a greater height. In the two-part dictionary definition quoted next, the term *small cottage* is offered up as a bungalow equivalent, and is in agreement with the first about the height of usually one story. Its second definition contains the more resolute pronouncement of having one story, which seems to preclude anything higher, and also suggests that this applies only to India. In consulting a third dictionary, another definition ventures to allow "sometimes an attic story," without being specific about whether or not the attic story may be used as actual living space, or only for storage. Which leads us to a final definition, perhaps the most widely accepted and understood, as well as easily interpreted. It allows a bungalow worthy of the name to have "up to one and one-half stories," thereby acknowledging at least the possibility, if not the likelihood, of using part of the attic as an additional room or two. This definition also implies that some, if not all of the bedrooms are on the main living level of the house, leaving the one-half story above as available for storage, until conversion to additional sleeping or other living space is required. For purposes of clarity and consistency, this particular definition is proposed as the most accurate, logical, and accommodating to how most bungalows were built, and for how most of them are still being

(*Opposite*) Detail of a bungalow interior in Pasadena, California. This pleasant corner of Lori King and David Heller's 1911 home shows how color can be the key to enlivening a modest bungalow's interior, while utilizing an authentic palette of the period. Still intact, the room's original wainscot was intended to imply the effect of more expensive wood paneling. It is created with vertical battens of dark-stained fir placed directly against the plaster and capped with a plate rail. Above, lightly sponged golden yellow walls provide a bright background for the objects set on the plate rail. The shades of the light fixture hanging in the foreground were the inspiration for the room's color scheme. The old Navajo rug on the floor, a vintage embroidered pillow on the Limbert rocker at the left, and a Gustav Stickley pillow design at right adapted by Dianne Ayres provide pattern, color, and texture to this welcoming Arts and Crafts interior.

lived in today. It is also the definition that may be applied to the majority of examples illustrated in this book. (Some related larger-scale houses have also been included, and are noted as such.)

Agreement about the linguistic origins of the term *bungalow* seems to be quite universal. The word as we know and spell it is an Anglo-Indian version of Bangala, which was the proper name of an old Hindu kingdom, renamed Bengal Presidency by the British, and was also used to describe a common form of rural Bengali hut. Initially, the word became assimilated into the English language by the early-nineteenth century, and was first used by British colonials, stationed in the remote outpost of Bengal, to describe housing built for them that was adapted from local traditions. As the century progressed the term took on a life of its own, and became associated with many different housing forms that were used to house the British and other foreign visitors throughout all of India. Some of these buildings were small, self-contained single-family homes designed for permanent occupancy. Others were compounds of similar individual structures that formed the Rest Houses or inns built by the British government, and located along the main roads of travel. Their common guest areas were contained in one larger building, while the kitchen facilities were placed in a separate structure, connected by a covered walkway. The actual guest accommodations were located in another structure, with bedrooms opening onto a long, straight corridor. These kinds of buildings were invariably single-story, with their prominent roofs usually sweeping low enough to cover the verandahs (or porches) that surrounded them. This roofline helped guide much of the heat upward, and any available breezes entered the interior through multiple open doors and windows that were shaded by the verandah's overhang. Like their original Bengalese forerunner, these anglicized versions worked because they still employed the same basic formula that had long proven effective in the sweltering Indian climate.

Gradually, the visual characteristics gleaned from the original Bangala became infused with influences from housing traditions elsewhere in India. Diverse sources, ranging from the utilitarian British army tent to the rural English cottage, also contributed their modifications. Spreading further out into the British Empire, related housing forms began appearing in such far-flung places as Ceylon, Kenya, Fiji, Australia, New Zealand, the Malay Peninsula, and other regions of Southeast Asia. Adaptations of different local building customs added further variety to examples in these places, but the basic formula remained quite constant: a modest single-story dwelling with a prominent roofline, verandah, and a centrally placed living room that helped to circulate air throughout the interior. The bungalow, for the English, became associated with the concept of a retreat from the foreign ways of the native societies that populated their colonial outposts. It was in this way that the bungalow began to acquire its enduringly rustic reputation, becoming known as a rural rather than an urban housing form, where the tranquility of nature's simpler pleasures beckoned. Idealized visions of pleasantly sited enclaves, such as those in the Himalayan foothills that provided seasonal relief from the scorching heat of the Indian plains, fed into a kind of escapist fantasy about bungalows that raised them beyond the level of mere cottages. There was an element of novelty in the concept of life in remote and untamed places, made habitable enough to host certain favorite traditions and pastimes of European civilization in relative safety and comfort. Such exotic settings were certainly to be admired for their natural beauty or perhaps for the study of local monuments, but the implication was one of cultural exclusivity in the name of the British Empire. The legacy of this association would contribute to the popularity and mystique that surrounded the appeal of the bungalow as it would evolve back home in England and even in America.

# Influences on the Bungalow

## AN OVERVIEW
## OF THE ARTS AND CRAFTS MOVEMENT

The Arts and Crafts Movement had its beginnings in England around the middle of the nineteenth century, and would prove to be a primary source of influence on the design and planning of many bungalows over half a century later. The familiar emphasis on handcrafted materials and objects in much of their architecture and interior design is a good example of this influence and its enduring appeal. The movement itself began to emerge when England was at her peak of world power as a center of industry and commerce, and the range of Queen Victoria's British Empire was never greater.

The Industrial Revolution was creating an element of conflict that was to become a basic factor toward the establishment of the Arts and Crafts Movement. This conflict was demonstrated by the far-reaching and controversial effects that mechanization was having on many manual skills and traditional crafts. To many small and specialized businesses or individual craftspeople, this trend was a threat to their way of life. To the larger business owners, who could benefit from machine-assisted manufacturing, the goals of growth and financial reward were at hand. The average factory worker welcomed the prospects of a reduction in physical drudgery made possible by new manufacturing methods. The availability of mass-produced household goods at reasonable cost seemed promising.

Various agendas concerning the advent of the machine age existed, but all would agree it was something to be reckoned with.

While today's working-world scenario of unemployment as a result of computer mechanization is a familiar one, different concerns and smaller numbers characterized the labor force that sustained the Industrial Revolution. Despite ongoing mechanization, workers were still needed to operate the new equipment, and perform many other tasks that might be taken up by automation or computers today. The average working-family's budget was helped by the availability of reasonably priced household goods. Although the business side of society was faring well, there were other costs of which the average working family may not have been aware. One was the increasing complication of urban social problems in the newly crowded cities. The poor were aggravated by abysmally low wages and cramped living conditions. The exploitation of overworked and underpaid immigrants, women, and child-age workers suggests that the moral priorities of many business owners were misplaced. Such pressing problems cried out for reform, but were often ignored or tolerated by those powerful enough to do something about them. Perceived by workers but seldom resolved to their satisfaction, the elements of greed and abuse in big business created time-bombs of unrest, and ultimately spawned unionization efforts to protect worker's rights. Compared to such issues, pondering the cultural price society would pay by allowing long-standing craft traditions to fall victim to assembly-line thinking and practice might seem a misplaced priority. To the impassioned few who understood its implications and heard its warning, this cause would help launch the Arts and Crafts Movement.

An important early voice for this message was John Ruskin (1819–1900), best known as a philosophical art critic, who also became successful as an influential teacher and writer of strong ideas and opinions. He is also known for his sympathy and support of the aims of a group of renegade artists who were attempting to reform accepted styles of academic painting in favor of a style, thought to be more vivid and honest, inspired by the Gothic or Medieval period. The group became known as the Pre-Raphaelite Brotherhood, because its work harkened back to "pre-Raphael" times, before the Renaissance introduced its foreign influence of classical painting to England. For a similar reason, Ruskin advocated the Gothic style as a flexible and suitable precedent for new architecture. He believed it to be a true English style that had lost its integrity and purity after the Italian influence arrived with the Renaissance. It was the legacy and influence of Ruskin that infused the feeling of the Gothic or Medieval into much of the design work of the English Arts and Crafts Movement. He believed that the effects of mass production essentially debased the former stature of the decorative arts, and in the process had also done the same bad turn to individual craftspeople. Citing the Middle Ages as having been an ideal time for the craftsperson, Ruskin advocated for the benefits of personal satisfaction to be gained by involvement in all phases of a craft, from design inception to final product, rather than merely somewhere along the way, as in a factory assembly line. The implication that some of society's ills might be cured by encouraging workers to develop a sense of personal pride and correspondingly diverse range of skills and responsibilities in their craft, is another one of the reforms that the Arts and Crafts Movement set out to accomplish.

Even though many of the scientific and mechanical innovations that contributed to the Industrial Revolution happened before 1800, most of its effects occurred well after the onset of the nineteenth century. Increased international trade and commerce, which also turned the wheels of industry, was expanding major world markets overseas. America was still in the early decades of its independence during this period, and continued to look to England as a model for much of its cultural and industrial development. Another major factor in economic growth was the rapid emergence of the railroad. So far-reaching were its effects on all of society that the impressive iron-and-glass train sheds of the Victorian era have been described as the "cathedrals of the nineteenth century." Their emblematic importance to the industry, commerce, and ingenuity of their day parallels the social, religious, and artistic significance of the great Gothic cathedrals to the Middle Ages.

In Victorian England, if an individual's sense of business and timing were up to the task, personal wealth became something that was actually possible to be earned, as opposed to the more traditional route of inheritance. Tremendous fortunes were indeed amassed by some, but the average person was usually satisfied to be gainfully employed, even if that involved working at menial and repetitive tasks in exchange for job security. Since industry required the labor of workers and the supervision of management, a kind of pecking order that characterized socio-economic levels of society was reflected in one's place and nature of employment. In England, the traditions of class distinction were sharply drawn, and if this was perceived as an unacceptable limitation, one way out was to consider relocation elsewhere. For the personally ambitious who had no useful connections at home, posting to one of the far reaches of the British Empire, such as Canada or Australia, may have offered some possibilities for advancement. America, with its mythic reputation as the proverbial land of opportunity, and its legend of the self-made man promoted by real-life success stories, was also a destination of choice.

In 1851, everyone seemed to be heading for London from just about everywhere. That was the year the Great

Exhibition of the Works of Industry of all Nations opened as the first international event of its kind, the forerunner of all subsequent World Fairs. Among its chief supporters was Prince Albert, consort of Queen Victoria, who took a strong personal interest in the event to ensure that it was a successful reflection of England's prosperity and its role as a leading world power. While better than half of its total exhibition space was devoted to British displays, many other countries, including the United States, joined in to showcase their own export products. As incentives to attract the best, official competitions were set up in which exhibitors vied for medals of recognition for their technical and even artistic achievements. It was a blockbuster of an event, with attendance surpassing the most hopeful expectations. The true showpiece of the Exhibition was the building that came to be known as the Crystal Palace, an immense iron-and-glass structure that surpassed in scale even the great train sheds. To fulfill a specific requirement of the architectural competition that inspired it, the machine-inspired modularity of the building's design allowed it to be dismantled and permanently reconstructed after the Exhibition as an enduring public attraction. It survived in a suburban London location until a fire destroyed it in 1936. The building's design was also a foreshadowing of more modern things to come, and represented a shift away from the historical-revival styles that characterized most architecture throughout the nineteenth century. In fact, the most progressive Victorian building designs tended to be commercial or industrial structures such as office buildings or warehouses, and it was America that would soon come to dominate achievements in those building types, as well as in new construction techniques.

England was still at the forefront of design and industry in 1851, with the Crystal Palace itself almost outdone by the dazzling array of machines and manufactured goods that were on display within. It is interesting to note that one of the Exhibition displays was a showcase of British-made goods in the Gothic Revival style called the Medieval Court, which was coordinated by Augustus Welby Northmore Pugin (1812–1852). An outspoken architect and designer whose philosophy in some ways paralleled Ruskin's beliefs, Pugin was also a working practitioner of the Gothic Revival style. Like Ruskin, he believed that the Gothic was the only style worthy of consideration as the national style of England, and was even more adamant about it. There was conflict between Pugin's insistent association of his adopted Roman Catholic faith with the Gothic style and Ruskin's views, which were staunchly Protestant. Although they disagreed on many issues, both felt that art and architecture had the capacity to redeem and improve society, a recurring theme of the Arts and Crafts Movement. Pugin's own career was dominated by ecclesiastical commissions, but he also produced superb designs for many related decorative arts that were displayed to much public acclaim in 1851 at the Medieval Court. His own work and ideas are often considered precursors to the aims of the English Arts and Crafts Movement. His approach to the use of the Gothic Revival style was one of respect and reverence toward its traditional craft aspects. His work demonstrated a sense of strict appropriateness in its applications to new forms in buildings, interiors, and objects. Subject to controversy in his life, he also published some notoriously opinionated books about the Gothic style that would contribute substance and direction to the Arts and Crafts Movement's philosophy and provide goals for many of the upcoming generation.

Pugin had recently completed a stunning collaboration with architect Sir Charles Barry on the reconstructed Houses of Parliament in London. Their finely crafted interiors and furnishings are one of his greatest achievements. His work on the Medieval Court in 1851 was one of his last projects, and later that year he wrote to an associate about his failing health, saying that he was "sure it was brought on by that detestable amount of Paganism in that exhibition."[3] Echoing Pugin's sentiments, this exhibition, in spite of its wide popularity, would later be characterized by others as having had a distinct lack of fine aesthetic design in most of its products and displays, which seemed overtly calculated to impress and tempt an unwary public with gaudy, superfluous, and inappropriate ornament. Pugin's criticism had been pointed, and some people were beginning to understand and accept that such a problem existed with many manufacturers. This dilemma came to be known as the conflict of "art vs. industry," or how the priority and importance of good design and workmanship was interpreted and played against the compellingly profitable appetite of the consumer market. The eager public, largely uneducated in matters of taste and consequently unaccustomed to giving strong priority to good design or even quality of materials in their purchases, were predictably tempted by fancy-looking goods of dubious quality. The socio-economic profile of society was changing rapidly, and most newly affluent consumers were far more acquisitive than discerning in their selections. Manufacturers were only too delighted to sell them products, whether in questionable taste or not, and they clearly weren't interested in preserving whatever craft traditions were being squeezed out of the market or undermined by the progress of the flourishing machine age.

Not all the voices of caution and reason considered the machine a hopeless intrusion on traditions of the past. There were some artistically progressive individuals who embraced the opportunities of mechanization, yet realized it could easily be misused, and sought to work toward its aesthetic redemption. Through their efforts the design-reform movement was inaugurated, and its goals were to educate the public about what constituted good quality in design and taste, as well as to improve the level of quality in the realm of manufactured goods. This sentiment eventually established and secured the need for competent industrial designers, professionally trained to understand new materials and manufacturing methods, and able to create well-designed products appropriate to the specialized requirements of mass production. A prominent English pioneer in this field was Christopher Dresser (1834–1904). He influenced both his peers and the public through his widely published design ideas. Dresser felt compelled to work with the machine rather than against it, and created, with great practical and aesthetic success, strikingly progressive designs in metal, glass, ceramics, and flat pattern that were well-suited for mass production. Dresser's achievements were an indication that machine production didn't necessarily preclude the element of quality in design, and remain a testimony to the timelessness of that concept.

Another English name associated with progressive design ideas was that of Charles Lock Eastlake (1836–1906), who is best known for his influential book *Hints on Household Taste*, first published in 1868, which helped to popularize the emerging concept of design-reform ideas. Like other early proponents of the Arts and Crafts Movement, he used the Gothic style as an ideal of the past that could be successfully reinterpreted in modern work. He contended that this reliance upon a rational design influence, with its traditions of linking structural form with ornament and its emphasis on honest use of materials, was the best way to achieve designs of quality and integrity, especially in furniture and interiors. The book was particularly popular in America and reprinted several times, spawning our own versions of Eastlake-style furniture and even architecture, most of which was ironically discredited by Eastlake himself as hopelessly inept, a debasement of what he had set out to accomplish, and unworthy of his name. Nevertheless, the name of Eastlake and the popularity of the style it created in America had indelibly entered the domain of popular culture.

Another movement that began in England, and had ties to design-reform thinking and the Arts and Crafts Movement was the Aesthetic Movement, which reached its peak in the 1870s and 1880s. Its reform aspects were more concerned with the concept of integrating art and beauty into daily living, rather than specifically preserving craft traditions or designing for machine production, although it was known actually to accommodate both. It was less clearly defined than the Arts and Crafts Movement in terms of ideology, although some of the finest designers of the day in both England and America were associated with it. The Aesthetic Movement even had an unofficial spokesperson in writer Oscar Wilde (1854–1900), an irrepressibly opinionated wit, who publi-

cized its concepts on the lecture circuit in America. Much of its design significance lay in how it popularized the use of certain motifs from exotic cultures, particularly that of Japan, into the design of new interiors and furnishings. Such motifs were perceived and promoted as a refreshing counterpoint to the overused staleness of most historic-revival styles, and Japan in particular would prove a rich and varied source of inspiration. In this way, it was progressive design, whose visual impact was strikingly different and perhaps even liberating from previous popular taste. Contributing to its appeal was the fact that the popularity of the Gothic Revival, even in its most progressive forms, was in decline as a domestic style. It was the Aesthetic Movement that promoted the concept of *artistic* interiors and furnishings, a term that implied the integration of handicrafts such as painting, embroidery, or porcelain into their design, and in that sense linked it to the Arts and Crafts Movement. With Oscar Wilde's pronouncements well publicized, it is not surprising that proponents of the Aesthetic Movement were often perceived as being snobbish and condescending toward middle-class taste, and they acquired a reputation as being intellectually pretentious and elitist.

Fashionable Aesthetic-style rooms favored delicate Japanesque designs in fabrics and art-wallpaper patterns, and established the wide popularity of the tripartite wall divisions of dado, filling, and frieze. To express further the occupant's good taste and sophistication, furniture forms of choice ranged from somewhat spindly, ebonized pieces in Anglo-Japanese style to variations of the so-called Eastlake style, as well as pieces with a Moorish or Middle Eastern influence.

Possibly the most famous room ever created in the Aesthetic taste is the sensational Peacock Room. It was designed by English architect Thomas Jeckyll (1827–1881) for the London home of wealthy shipping magnate Frederick Leyland, as an appropriate dining-room setting for his extensive collection of valuable Oriental blue-and-white porcelain that was then very much in vogue. It was only after the involvement of expatriate American painter James Abbott McNeill Whistler (1834–1903), who felt compelled to "improve" its design to be more compatible with one of his paintings to be displayed above its fireplace, that the room took on a life of its own. The painting, appropriately enough, was entitled *La Princesse du Pays de la Porcelaine*. It seems that while Leyland was conveniently out of town for a number of months, Whistler decided that it was necessary to take some artistic license by painting over some antique tooled-leather wall panels that Leyland prized, and incorporated some rather outlandish designs of peacocks in blue and gold instead. While the room is now considered a landmark of its style, the subsequent confrontations between artist and client over the unauthorized liberties taken with it made sensational news, and perhaps served Whistler better because of the colorful publicity than any satisfaction Leyland might have experienced as a result. The room was later purchased in its entirety, dismantled, reconstructed, and recently restored at the Smithsonian's Freer Gallery in Washington, D.C., where it is permanently installed.

As popular culture assimilated its quirks and reputation, the Aesthetic Movement became increasingly subject to misinterpretation and even satire. In its later phases, most of the original aims and aspirations of the movement became obscured through overexposure of the Aesthetic look in cheaply mass-produced and mediocre designs. It is, however, considered a forerunner to the Art Nouveau style, which also had Oriental influences.

Art Nouveau represented a clear departure from historicism, and it was the last of the progressive-design movements started in the nineteenth century, with links to the evolving Arts and Crafts Movement, especially in England. The style appeared mostly in pattern and graphic design there, and to some extent in the detailing of decorative arts, rather than in overall architectural and furniture forms, as it did in continental Europe. Notable is the work of a group of progressive designers in Glasgow, Scotland, especially that of architect Charles Rennie Mackintosh (1868–1928) around the turn of the century. The work of the Glasgow School shows evidence of the Art Nouveau influence, as well as that of Japan, but moved these influences in new directions. The craft tradition was strong in Scotland, too, and a thriving range of decorative arts was produced during this period. Mackintosh's own decorative work incorporates many of the motifs, such as the Glasgow Rose, which are associated with progressive Scottish design. Mackintosh took significant architectural inspiration from traditional Scottish building forms and materials, combining them with a sense of spare geometry that was offset by sleek, attenuated curves. His decorative-arts work is characterized by a light scale and sculptural form, with few direct references to historicism, and is often considered a precursor to the Modern Movement. He achieved a uniquely fresh style, and was ironically more influential in Europe than in Britain or America, particularly on the progressive Vienna Secessionist Movement that also was under way at the turn of the century.

Pride in the long-standing tradition of handmade crafts in England since the Middle Ages contributed to a sense of urgency that they must be saved as important achievements of civilization. These endangered crafts included all of the decorative arts: furniture, woven and printed textiles and needlework, glass, ceramics, and metalwork. In addition, the design and creation of decorative-painting schemes for interiors, architectural stone and woodcarving, and pattern design for textiles and wallpapers were important categories to consider. As suggested by the Crystal Palace, even the discipline of architecture itself was moving away from traditional design, construction, and materials. This was yet another area that was to be targeted for reform, and one resulting influence that the Arts and Crafts Movement had on domestic architecture is seen in many bungalow designs of early-twentieth-century America.

At the forefront of this movement's beginnings was William Morris (1834–1896), a visionary writer, poet, designer, craftsperson, and in later life a fervent socialist. A student of Ruskin's at Oxford, he soon abandoned his initial plans to become a clergyman and began to study architecture instead, only to switch again to the study of painting. It is notable that Morris was drawn into this study through the influence of painter and poet Dante Gabriel Rossetti (1828–1882), who happened to be one of the founding members of the Pre-Raphaelite Brotherhood. Morris himself became involved with this group, and was even enlisted by Rossetti with several of the others to collaborate on a large-scale interior painting scheme in the new Union Debating Hall at Oxford in 1857. Morris was also profoundly influenced by the teachings and writings of Ruskin. These would color his thoughts and direction about art, craft, and design throughout his lifetime. His career became more settled and focused after his marriage to a striking young woman named Jane Burden, who looked the very picture of brooding Pre-Raphaelite beauty, and was later painted and photographed as such by Rossetti.

Morris, who was moderately well-off and could afford to put some of the ideas gleaned from his studies to the test, undertook his own collaboration with a group of like-minded friends to construct and furnish a residence of his own, the Red House, in 1859. Morris also saw a practical application of a number of Ruskin's ideas in the successful way the project came together. Designed by Philip Webb (1831–1915), and located not far from London at Bexleyheath in Kent, the reddish-brick structure synthesized long-standing, local building traditions in its design, materials, and construction methods. Its significance lay in the fact that it wasn't merely a revival of yet another historic style, but a new design that adapted elements from the past in an appropriate way, yet remained sensitive to the integrity of its sources. The house has become a kind of icon of the beginnings of the English Arts and Crafts Movement, and embodies many of the ideas imparted by both Ruskin and Pugin.

Finding virtually all the household goods available in stores to be tasteless and inappropriate, Morris and his cohorts proceeded to furnish the interiors of the Red House with a range of handmade and handpainted furnishings that took their Ruskinian inspiration from the Middle Ages, but like the house itself, were new interpretations rather than historic copies. Encouraged by the success of their venture, Morris and friends collaborated again in 1861, this time to establish a collective business that would support the preservation of craft skills as part of a commercial enterprise. First called Morris, Marshall, Faulkner and Company after its core group of founders, it is best known by the name of Morris and Company, as it was renamed after reorganization in 1875. Its initial goal was to produce high-quality, handmade goods for the interior at a price most people could afford. It is ironic that this affordability was never truly achieved. Such good intentions weren't very practical for the financial health of the company, for the extra labor costs incurred to produce most of the goods dictated higher than average prices simply to break even. When it comes to the procurement of high-quality, handcrafted goods, the perennial adage that "you get what you pay for" seems to have been as true then as it is today. Called The Firm by its members, Morris and Company marketed its line of goods to the retail market, and also offered a complete in-house capability for custom interiors, including design concept and coordination, as well as the ability to fabricate and install all elements of the project.

Morris found his métier to be an ability to create appealing designs derived from nature for the hand-printed fabrics and wallpapers for which the company became famous. Philip Webb actually designed the first version of what has become widely known as the Morris chair, and it was a consistently popular item in the company's product line. Adapted from a basic concept found in some early adjustable furniture of seventeenth-century England, the name Morris is often generically applied to any such chair of generous scale, having a high, movable back that can be adjusted to several different angles by moving a supporting wooden or metal bar to various positions. This chair type would become a mainstay of the Arts and Crafts era and has inspired many stylistic variations, as did the bungalow itself. The company was also well known for their exceptional stained glass, and received many commissions for ecclesiastical projects. Other important departments were those concerning textiles, especially traditional tapestry design and weaving, embroidery, and woodblock-printed textiles. A company workshop was set up in 1880 to weave hand-knotted rugs at Hammersmith, just outside London. After early attempts to produce woodblock-printed wallpapers proved problematic, their printing was thereafter handled by Jeffrey and Company of London. The last venture of Morris's life was the Kelmscott Press, established in 1890, that produced masterful examples of fine art-book printing and binding. The Firm continued on with its high standards of quality work until it was finally dissolved in 1940, a remarkable track record for a company founded on such idealistic principles. Morris and Company employed some of the finest artisans and craftspeople in England,

and kept a core group of them steadily supplied with work.

Using the traditional craft skills that had come close to becoming obsolete, the production process also rekindled the opportunity of continuing those skills through apprenticeships for aspiring craftspeople. If not from a financial viewpoint, the artistic and moral success of Morris and Company's enterprise would prove to have a far-reaching influence, both in England and America. It inspired a number of similar ventures over the next few decades, reviving and updating the tradition of career involvement in a craft guild as a viable alternative for those who couldn't fathom being stuck in an office or factory for most of their lives. Important among its followers in England was the Century Guild, established in 1882 by Arthur Heygate Mackmurdo (1851–1942) and Selwyn Image (1849–1930), as well as the Guild of Handicraft, started in 1888 by Charles Robert Ashbee (1863–1942). Although more of a professional organization or club than a business itself, The Art Worker's Guild was founded in 1884 by a group of working artists, architects, designers, and craftspeople seeking to provide a forum for discussion and related lectures on various craft techniques and styles. Among its early members were the distinguished names of Morris, Mackmurdo, and Ashbee, as well as important English architects Richard Norman Shaw (1831–1912), Charles F. Annesley Voysey (1857–1941), and Edwin Lutyens (1869–1944). First developed as part of the Art Worker's Guild to organize its public exhibitions, a spin-off group called The Arts and Crafts Exhibition Society was formed in 1888, and continued to showcase the current work of craft-revival designers until the outbreak of World War I.

The message of Morris and his followers was heard in America, and one of its strongest proponents was Gustav Stickley (1858–1942). A trained stonemason, furniture maker, and metalworker who was born in Wisconsin, Stickley set out on a fateful visit to Europe in 1898, meeting Ashbee and Voysey in England, and absorbing what he could of the Arts and Crafts Movement there. He returned inspired, and soon established his own guild in the form of a furniture workshop in Eastwood, New York, which he called United Crafts, and then was renamed the Craftsman Workshops after it was expanded in 1900. Beyond the production of furniture, Stickley's compulsion to spread the message of Morris and his ideals throughout America found form in the publishing of his magazine, *The Craftsman* (1901–1916), which became a nationally prominent mouthpiece for progressive Arts and Crafts ideals. It was also a trend-setting resource, providing invaluable guidance through articles and examples that showed how to incorporate some of those ideals into daily living. In the earliest years, Stickley was in sympathy with the socialistic thinking that Morris had promoted, and published articles by prominent socialist writers concerning the state of modern social and economic conditions. Sensing the timeliness of their messages to America, he also publicized the philosophical and artistic contributions of Morris and Ruskin to the Arts and Crafts Movement, for this country's mood of social, economic, and design reform was growing at the turn of the century.

Within a few years, Stickley moved away from promoting socialist ideals, and also came to understand and accept the role of the machine in furniture production. While machines were found to be essential in producing his furniture in a timely and cost-effective manner, Stickley still employed hand-finishing techniques, natural materials, and in lieu of most ornament, an approach to design detailing that mostly featured sturdy-looking structural elements for visual interest. The best known and most significant side to Stickley's efforts was the promotion of what he referred to as the Craftsman style, which not only applied to furniture, but exerted a strong influence on related interior-design concepts and domestic architectural planning.

*The Craftsman* magazine became a national forum of ideas that informed and instructed readers on the practical and enduring wisdom of the Craftsman style as a way of life. The periodical showcased the work of many architects working in the Arts and Crafts mode around the country, including Greene and Greene and others in California, which in turn promoted that state as an ideal place to embrace the desirable combination of indoor/outdoor living that its mild climate made possible. Stickley himself designed not only furnishings and interiors but entire houses, and stressed the importance of harmony between a house and its landscape. The publication of photographs, drawings, and floorplans of houses became a major part of Stickley's marketing efforts, and he began selling complete house plans by mail. This practice would also be avidly pursued by many others, and have a major impact on the proliferation of bungalows constructed across the country. Attesting to their growing popularity, designs for Craftsman bungalows were featured prominently by Stickley, along with larger Craftsman-style homes, as new ideals of American domestic architecture.

When Stickley visited California in 1904, the remains of the old Spanish Colonial Missions and their harmony with the adjacent landscape impressed him. Soon the Mission style was perceived as being in rapport with the Craftsman style, and examples of its use were seen in the pages of *The Craftsman* as well as elsewhere, both in and beyond California. Subsequently, the term *Mission* came into popular usage, and like the bungalow itself, its meaning became subject to varying interpretations. It is notable that many design variations of Craftsman and Mission styles would be appropriated by others, who were keenly aware of Stickley's popularity and influence, and more than willing to capitalize on it. In a sense, Stickley became a victim of his own success. As competition was quick to appear on both the furniture and housing forefronts, his market share was cut into deeply after only a few years. Perhaps on some levels his own business sense was less suited to running the Craftsman empire than it was in communicating its philosophy. After filing for bankruptcy that was propelled by an overcommitment in a real-estate venture, Stickley's company was officially taken over in 1915 by his brothers Leopold and John George. They had left Gustav's Craftsman Workshops in 1900, when they are known to have executed some furniture designs for Frank Lloyd Wright at their own workshop in Fayetteville, New York. A sometimes confusing but notable family fact is that two other brothers, George and Albert, were also in the furniture business, and in 1891 established the Stickley Brothers Company in Grand Rapids, Michigan. Yet another brother, Charles, had established a partnership with an uncle in a New York state furniture business in 1889. Of all the Stickley brothers, however, it was Gustav's vision and ideas, as well as his magazine, that made the greatest contribution to the American Arts and Crafts Movement, and he is the one that is most linked to it. After his company was taken over, it was operated as The Stickley Manufacturing Company. Its descendant today goes by the name of L. & J.G. Stickley, Incorporated, and is still producing Arts and Crafts-style furniture to original period designs. It is also notable that one of Gustav Stickley's own homes, built as an agricultural compound called Craftsman Farms in Parsippany, New Jersey, is now under restoration as a museum and study center devoted to his contributions to American culture.

Another major contribution to the Arts and Crafts Movement in America was made by the Roycroft community, founded in 1895 in East Aurora, New York, by a charismatic figure named Elbert Hubbard (1856–1915). Like Gustav Stickley, Hubbard had journeyed to England and was impressed by achievements of the Arts and Crafts Movement. He had recently decided to end a successful career with The Larkin Company (for which the administration building was designed by Frank Lloyd Wright 1903–1905), where almost twenty years earlier he began as a founding partner of what had become a major manufacturer of soaps and toiletries in Buffalo, New York. After resigning in 1893, Hubbard's initial aspirations lay in writing and publishing his own books and periodicals. His visit to William Morris's Kelmscott Press at Hammersmith, England, in 1894 was an inspiring one, and he returned home to establish the Roycroft Press. (The name is derived from that of two English bookbinders of the seventeenth century, Samuel and Thomas Roycroft.) Having first published a periodical called *The Philistine* in 1895, its first book, *The Song of Songs*, was published by the Roycroft Press the following year and featured illustrations by Hubbard's first wife, Bertha.

It seems that the concept of the Roycroft community as

it would evolve was not entirely planned, but grew incrementally as opportunities beyond those of printing and publishing became apparent. It wouldn't be long before the idea of a community of craftspeople, working in close proximity and representing a comprehensive range of craft disciplines, would begin to take shape.

A dynamic and enterprising man, Hubbard possessed considerable business acumen and experience that helped keep the financial side of his new enterprise in order. The marketing skills he developed over the years at the Larkin Company would prove to be invaluable to the development of the Roycroft community. With this in mind it isn't surprising that Hubbard, encouraged by the success of his publications, also found a convenient source of supplemental funds by going on lecture tours across the country. By the turn of the century, the Roycroft enterprise had already expanded to include 175 workers, and a multiacre campus was in the process of being assembled and expanded through the annexation of several adjacent properties. At its peak, the total work force comprised over 500 people. A building campaign was underway that would eventually include a diverse range of workshops, worker housing, visitor accommodations, and other related structures that would physically define the Roycrofter's domain. Starting with a Print Shop building, Hubbard soon added a towered stone Chapel, and proceeded to construct a worker's dormitory to supplement existing housing on some adjacent properties. The Roycroft Inn was first constructed in 1903, but was expanded several times over the next decade to accommodate an increasing stream of visitors. This influx was encouraged by the staging of several annual conventions on various themes, featuring subjects and guest speakers of interest to existing or prospective Roycroft clientele. The fame and reputation of the community was spreading in ways that paralleled those used by Hubbard in his previous career successes.

Expansion of the campus continued, producing a Blacksmith (later Copper) Shop, Furniture Shop, and another large housing structure for personnel that included recreational facilities shared by guests. The range of crafts produced by the Roycrofters was comprehensive. In addition to their metalwork, printing, bookbinding, and furniture departments, there was also the Roycroft Modelled Leather Department. With such a range of crafts and facilities, it isn't surprising that the community attracted and sustained a wide range of high-quality craftspeople. In turn, they promoted the continuity of their craft traditions through apprenticeships, as was typical of other craft-guild organizations. In true community spirit there was the sharing of personnel between departments, which served to ease sporadic workload requirements, as well as to provide employees with opportunities to become skilled in more than one craft. There were a number of accomplished painters, sculptors, and photographers who were also associated with the community over the years. The sense of unity created by Hubbard and his associates came close to fulfilling a kind of utopian dream of the Arts and Crafts Movement that was seldom achieved or sustained for long elsewhere.

In 1915, an era was ended when Elbert Hubbard and his second wife Alice were lost in the fateful sinking of the liner *Lusitania* by a German submarine. Hubbard's eldest son, Elbert II ("Bert"), assumed the leadership of the community and it survived the tragedy, but eventually changing times and Depression-era economics led to its closure in 1938. Purchased in 1939 by Samuel Guard, a publisher of agricultural magazines, there was some hope that it could remain intact under his auspices. However, within that year Guard was impelled to dispose of property and buildings that weren't related to his printing business, and the remaining portions of the campus were subsequently sold off piecemeal to various owners. Today, a large number of its structures survive intact, including a 1910 Roycroft-built house that now functions as the Elbert Hubbard Museum and the Roycroft Inn, newly revitalized in time for the community's centennial year. By arrangement with the present-day L. & J.G. Stickley, Inc., some original Roycroft furniture designs have also been reissued.

Architect Frank Lloyd Wright (1867–1959) had an extraordinarily long career, but his works, for the most part, existed outside of the mainstream of the American architectural world and public taste. His early career involvement in the development of the Prairie style coincides with the arrival of the Arts and Crafts Movement in America, and has some connections to it. The term *Prairie* was derived from a French word for an extensive meadow, and here it refers to the spreading lines of the Midwestern landscape, a guiding force in the creation of architecture appropriate to it. The style is characterized by a strong horizontality expressed through deep roof overhangs, open, spreading floorplans, and often outdoor terraces that link the structure to its site. Building materials are sturdy, durable, and suitable for the harsh climate. Brick and concrete predominate, with stucco and wood also seen on exteriors. Rooflines, usually shallow and hipped to reduce verticality, sometimes appear almost flat. The relative spareness and severity about many Prairie designs suggest a proto-modern feeling with its geometric influence. It was quite a departure from the common historical-revival styles that still dominated America at the turn of the century. From the outside, the Prairie houses seldom appeared quaint or cozy, but they emerged stylistically as uniquely American.

It is significant that Wright and other proponents of the Prairie style were among the charter members of the Chicago Arts and Crafts Society founded in 1897. In 1901, he presented a manifesto called "The Art and Craft of the Machine," in which he praised Morris, but argued that the machine, if correctly used, was the very means by which the same essential goals of Morris could be achieved. Although he embraced natural materials as ideal, Wright felt that their manipulation by a machine could be aesthetically acceptable, and even used to achieve an inspired result. Wright's opinionated pronouncements would distance him from the mainstream, yet his influence would affect many people.

Wright's training was grounded in progressive thinking, and it was the influence of architect Louis Sullivan (1856–1924) that led him toward the concept that all design, whether of ornament or architecture, was founded upon the laws of nature. Wright had worked in Sullivan's office, a progressive and creative place where mostly commercial commissions had helped pioneer the use of steel framing in early versions of the skyscraper. Sullivan was brilliant at the integration of organically inspired ornament into an overall architectural context, which inspired Wright. Although it would take many forms, a strong sense of the organic would appear in Wright's work throughout his career. Planning devices used by Wright and other architects to express their Prairie-style designs are similar to those seen in many bungalows, but are most readily seen in their interiors. They share the concept of free-flowing interior spaces, to expand visually the main living areas. The symbolic central physical importance of the fireplace to the home is another. Wright was known almost to enshrine the fireplace, emphasizing its importance through exaggerated scale or with built-in seating. As in the typical bungalow, Prairie designers favored built-ins such as windowseats and dining-room sideboards that reduced the likelihood of inappropriately furnished or cluttered rooms.

Seen in virtually all bungalow design is the pronounced feeling of horizontality that is typically also expressed on the Prairie exterior. Inside the Prairie house, this feeling was often accentuated by lower ceilings with beams or very linear molding placement, rhythmic bands of windows grouped together, and squared-off woodwork of sometimes chunky proportions. Many Prairie-style houses also featured leaded art glass, usually quite geometric, that was well integrated with the whole scheme. Similar art-glass designs are seen in many bungalows. A critical difference between the kind of Prairie houses that Wright designed and the bungalow examples that echoed the style, was a matter of scale and cost. Wright designed for an affluent clientele on a custom, one-of-a-kind basis during this period. The average bungalow was both modestly scaled and priced, probably built of mass-produced parts, and most often its actual architect or designer was unknown or unimportant to its occupants. In Wright-designed Prairie houses, the interiors would be completely integrated with the architecture through materials, lighting, and appropri-

ately scaled and placed furniture of his design. In most bungalows, however, the furnishings and interior design often evolved piecemeal, as its occupants could afford or were inspired to implement. The decorating bibles for bungalow design ideas were related books and national periodicals such as *House Beautiful, House and Garden*, or perhaps *The Craftsman* magazine. Wright was already moving away from his Prairie period after 1910, but the style would continue elsewhere well into the 1920s, and would be incorporated into many anonymous bungalow designs.

Despite their common ground, what was the genesis of the relationship between the Prairie style and the bungalow? It is difficult to evaluate conclusively, and it could be argued either way that one was an influence on the other. What can be certain is that both entities are firmly established and recognized as distinctive American achievements, and they were most likely mutually influential forces. Even after Wright outgrew it, the Prairie style managed to retain its modern image. Its strong contrast to the more overtly picturesque styles that still had an ongoing appeal in the bungalow market kept it highly visible, only to be eclipsed by the more extreme severity of the International Style after 1930.

The Arts and Crafts Movement found its limited, but devoted, following in America probably because it showed a path of tangible expression toward an idealistic goal. Life and the world at large could be made better through dedication, hard work, and perseverance. It offered many things to believe in, to accomplish, and to aspire to. It gave new meaning to life for some at a time when the individual was losing a sense of self in the context of the world at large. Its obvious success was in getting people to care about something. To believe that the Arts and Crafts Movement could change the world was also to believe, to paraphrase Anne Frank, "that people are basically good at heart," and that not everyone was just out to "make a buck" for himself. There were principles, goals, and aspirations to live up to, even if they were at odds with the industrial machine that had the world under its spell. The fact that the Movement existed at all demonstrated that there were at least enough people around to agree collectively to make a difference in and even change what was perceived as a deplorable situation. In contrast, the fact that much of the rest of the population was either somewhere on the fence or even opposed to the Arts and Crafts cause was a challenge to its basic existence. Yet, even if good intentions don't pay the bills, does that mean we shouldn't still have them? This dilemma of the heart and mind troubled many people who were deeply committed to the cause. Some kept the faith in spite of adversity, and learned to live with the dichotomy of the situation. After all, perhaps the key to happiness in life was to be found in the process, not the result, of one's efforts. In other words, keep your nose to the grindstone. Life is what you make it. If these gems of philosophy sound like classic Americanisms or echoes of the Protestant Work Ethic, they are indeed. That may explain part of why the ideals of the Movement struck so close to home to some hopeful Americans. Most devotees were enterprising and energetic people with commitment in their blood, and that is exactly what the Arts and Crafts Movement needed to keep going and get something done. We have seen that some even made rather successful careers of it. But, like other causes, it on occasion tended toward smug self-righteousness. Some of its goals, methods, and proselytizing offended a few and alienated others who perhaps could have been allies. But it also inspired a dedicated core to carry on and make a difference. It was blessed with inspiring leaders of great magnetism and intelligence, and without them it couldn't have gotten off the ground, let alone inspire worldwide admiration, awe, and study almost a century later.

A few of America's greatest achievements in the realm of the Arts and Crafts Movement have been mentioned here, but there were so many more. The caliber of the decorative arts produced at many different craft enterprises across the country was exceptional, and always distinctively American, despite its original English inspiration. The artistic triumphs of American art pottery, tiles, and other ceramics are legendary. Our furniture, metalwork, glass, and textile arts also define a significant part of the Arts and Crafts Movement worldwide. The vigorous and active revival of the Movement, long building and now flowering again in all its disciplines, is remarkably strong, and holds much promise. Only a small sampling of these arts and of the achievements of American architecture and interior design of the period is highlighted in this book. It is intended to showcase them, but also to serve as an indication of how much more is out there. Certainly, the distinctive realm of the Arts and Crafts house has only begun to be explored, rediscovered, and savored. As it nears its second century on our landscape, the vintage qualities of Arts and Crafts design embodied in the bungalow may be said to be aging well.

# The Bungalow Arrives in America

## WELCOME HOME

The first documented example of an American building described as a bungalow, a summer house on Cape Cod, Massachusetts, appeared in the *American Architect and Building News* in 1880. Another early example of the term's use was published in 1884 by A.W. Brunner in *Cottages or Hints on Economical Building*, describing a small gabled and dormered house with multiple porches that could otherwise be termed a Queen Anne-style cottage.[4] Prior to these examples, the word must have been assimilated into the American vocabulary by means of travel, or perhaps through its mention in popular literature. A consistent planning format was emerging, however, that would continue to characterize bungalows in America.

The bungalow's initial link with American vacation architecture is significant, as it came to be associated with leisure, informality, and natural settings through its early "summer-cottage" incarnation. Although outward appearances of houses called bungalows varied, the Shingle style was often used at seaside locations. With roots in the American vernacular architecture of colonial farm buildings, the Shingle style also had received some significant influences from England's version of the Queen Anne style. The beginnings of the Shingle style were first interpreted in domestic architecture by the important architect Henry Hobson Richardson (1838–1886) in the William Watts Sherman house in Newport, Rhode Island, in 1874.

Richardson is actually better known for establishing his Richardsonian Romanesque style as a vehicle of progressive design, which uses the vocabulary of its historic namesake in a new way. His use of the Romanesque Revival style forms a parallel to the more progressive uses of the Gothic Revival style in England. He pivotally affected the direction of American architecture in the late-nineteenth century through his landmark commissions for Trinity Church of 1876 in Boston and the Marshall Field Wholesale Building of 1885–1887 in Chicago. It is notable that Richardson was a particularly major influence on Louis Sullivan, as well as Frank Lloyd Wright. An interesting observation involves one of his works, the Ames Memorial Gate Lodge in North Easton, Massachusetts, of 1880–1881, which gives a strikingly rustic quality to Romanesque Revival forms through its use of massive and irregular granite boulders found in the area. Richardson's use of this natural "found" building material makes a compelling comparison to a similar use of "found" boulders and river rock in many California bungalow designs of over three decades later.

The Adirondack style, which incorporated rustic, unfinished wood and log detailing, was popular in mountainous resort areas (figs. 3, 53). The style was named after the mountain range in New York State, which was a fashionable summer-resort area established in the nineteenth century as a getaway from the sweltering heat of the East Coast. In the Adirondacks are many examples of the style, and its name has also become widely associated with a perennially popular style of outdoor lawn chair, which fea-

1. A Craftsman-style bungalow in Berkeley, California. Constructed in 1909 for the sum of $1,950 by local builder Carl Eriksson, this house shows an Oriental influence in its upswept gable peak. Attributed to plans ordered from Sears, Roebuck and Company, this design is nevertheless nearly identical to one in a plan book by Henry L. Wilson (fig. 2). The clinker-brick porch piers are typical, but the mortise-and-tenon detailing of the paired columns is reminiscent of Arts and Crafts furniture designs. Note the window flanked by ventilation louvers in the gable peak.

tures broad planks of wood to form its back, arms, and seat. Mountain resort areas, made accessible by the advent of train travel from the cities, developed in a number of New England states, as well as the mid-Atlantic region. Virtually all of these areas had similar architectural forms that celebrated rusticity and informality. Concurrently, our system of National Parks was emerging, and the Adirondack style would strongly influence the lodges and cabins that would proliferate in and near them. The widespread use of closely related styles was seen in the National Parks and resort areas of the Rocky Mountain states, as well as those further west and north on the Pacific coast.

With the national icon of the log cabin familiar to most people, it is not surprising that the rusticity of the Adirondack style was readily accepted as suitable for American vacation architecture. Many expressions of this style were actually family compounds that usually featured one large lodge-like structure as a central gathering place for meals, socializing, and perhaps outside-visitor accommodations. Surrounding this were smaller separate cabins that were used by various branches of the family. If not a privately owned family compound, much the same arrangement existed at other camps, where individual families could rent cabins for the season. Publicly accessible camps didn't always have a central lodge, and often the cabin was self-sufficient for the family who rented it. While it seems that *cabin* was the preferred term for small houses in mountain locations, they often possessed the requisite physical criteria to have been called bungalows.

Vacation architecture that was adjacent to the ocean developed somewhat differently, and the more modest vacation homes tended to be more closely situated in village-like communities that offered a choice of other accommodations such as larger hotels and guest houses. Besides the Shingle style, other simple interpretations of colonial-derived housing forms found favor, often with clapboard siding. Many middle-class families could afford to own second homes, and by the turn of the century, entire seasonal communities existed in many different beauty spots, not all of them in the mountains or at the beach. In midwestern locations, most cities were within reasonable distance of a picturesque lake or river setting that fostered such resort development. As in the mountains, many seacoast or lakeside summer homes were technically bungalows, and some of them were labeled as such. The inconsistencies in America concerning what to label one's small house are probably due to upbringing, habit, and personal taste. Different words bring up different associations, and for many years people were simply more used to hearing such small houses described as cottages. Perhaps this is one of the reasons that "bungalow" became such a buzzword in American popular culture for a time. With all its associated lore, hype, and philosophy, the term

was destined to become something more than just another generic name for a small house, like cabin and cottage seem to be.

Despite the various forms that American domestic vacation architecture assumed, there were many consistencies between them that also echo bungalow-planning concepts. First among these is the connection to their setting, and location was a central factor in vacation housing. Once the getaway spot of choice was established, the requirements of the building were easier to define. The basic premise of such a house was to address the informal needs of the family at leisure. Its planning needed to accommodate the basic family unit in a comfortable way, as well as to allow adequate space for impromtu family gatherings involving larger groups. The out-of-doors invariably entered the picture as an extension of the house, often through attached decks or adjacent ground-level picnic areas or other open spaces close to the mountains, woods, and lake, or beach and ocean.

Although leisure time and summer activities were the main draw of the summer home, most middle-class resort areas meant that crowds of people were never too far away. The idea of a real retreat to a truly private place appealed to many people, but few could afford it. This situation is somewhat comparable to that of the bungalow neighborhood, where in many developments the houses are so close together that they lose the garden-setting associations that the best of the bungalows exemplify. Nevertheless, with some imagination and the right state of mind, even crowded conditions can be overlooked in favor of the "good things to be thankful for." This was the credo that nurtured the American Dream of home ownership, along with the idea that after all, no matter what form the home was, it was one's own private domain and castle.

On a lesser scale, the same idea applied to vacation houses, which were also personal symbols of achievement and security to their owners. Many renters took pride in being able to afford to return to the same vacation home year after year, and loved it like their own. Similarly, most middle-class people were glad they could even afford to own a summer place. Modest as some of the vacation architecture had to be, there still was a certain element of indulgence in the whole concept. Most families took great pleasure in being able to share their summer homes with others, such as "poor relations" who couldn't afford the same thing on their own.

Screen-enclosed porches, used for sleeping as well as living spaces, contributed to the necessary flexibility of being able to provide extra guest accommodations for such visitors at short notice. This informality was reflected in a distinct lack of traditionally separate living and dining rooms, and often combined both functions into one large space where all the shared indoor activities could take

13

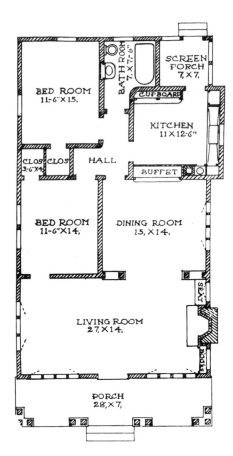

2. A Craftsman-style bungalow and floorplan. This design was offered in an undated plan book called *Wilson's California Bungalow*, published by a Los Angeles architect named Henry L. Wilson, who coined "The Bungalow Man" as his sobriquet. Selling many such plans by mail, he also published the West Coast monthly, *Bungalow Magazine*, between 1909 and 1918, which helped to promote his plan business. This floorplan reveals a characteristically space-efficient house, with a generous front porch, leading directly into a large living room with fireplace, which is open to the dining room. Other typical features, such as multiple built-ins, bedrooms on the same level, a compact kitchen, and handy service areas illustrate the livable and practical appeal of bungalow planning.

3. A front porch furnished as an "outdoor living room." An illustration from Henry L. Saylor's book called *Bungalows* (1911), this front porch is furnished with many indoor amenities, yet embraces nature in its open-air setting. The columns of this porch, which are made from natural tree trunks, show the influence of the Adirondack style.

4. A living room with an open attic-loft area. Using examples such as this, Henry Saylor's *Bungalows* was one of several design-advice books that helped to define public taste about how to plan, build, and furnish such houses. This room, probably in a vacation house, has a large fireplace as its focalpoint, and the cozy and informal atmosphere of the room characterizes many bungalow interiors.

place. Bedrooms were usually quite small, and as numerous as space would allow. Concerns about adequacy of furnishings and facilities were minimal at best, since nobody would have to put up with things for too long anyway. There was an element of pleasurable adventure in making do or roughing it, especially if life at home was rigidly defined and disciplined. As with bungalows, the majority of the open space in the interior was devoted to the main living area, which often took on something of the character of a lodge in its style of furnishings (fig. 4). Convenience, thrift, and practicality usually ruled the choices here, and often a family's cast-offs from home would find their way to their vacation house. Although this practice was renounced in design-advice books as an idea that should be avoided, people generally didn't take readily to such controlling pretenses as aesthetics when it came to putting together their own second home.

Although the bungalow had actually already arrived in nineteenth-century America, relatively few people realized it until after 1900. It was only in the years soon to follow that the term became a household word, and quickly became a permanent part of the American culture. The bungalow had indeed come home in the sense that it found form here like nowhere else, and early-twentieth-century America welcomed it with open arms.

# Marketing the Bungalow

### A BIG BUSINESS FOR A SMALL HOUSE

The "bungalow business," which was fueled by the proliferation of literature that promoted it, became a considerable industry. While a significant amount of the publicity was found in such periodicals as *The Ladies Home Journal, House Beautiful,* or *The Craftsman* magazine, the major bungalow promotion was done with house-plan books. Some of these resembled catalogs, for they had soft covers, were printed in black and white, and had only a few sketchy renderings of the house plans themselves. Others were artfully designed coffee-table books, with glowing prose and stylish color renderings of the various dream houses contained within. Many presentations, aspiring to an upscale clientele, included color renderings of interiors with fashionably dressed and coiffed occupants posed here and there. With promotion a priority in a competitive market, publishers of these plan books were sometimes even willing to give them away, in the hope of securing the modest price of about $5 to $25 for a complete set of house plans (figs. 2, 16, 19). For a small additional fee, the plans could be easily modified or adapted to suit a house lot.

While there was always the chance that some frugal buyers would just give a page from the plan book to a builder, or adapt the house plan themselves on the site, most consumers were convinced of the wisdom of purchasing a complete plan. The designs were typically done by anonymous draftsmen, but some plans can be traced to a specific designer or architect, and most of the houses published in design or building periodicals and books were so credited. Perhaps the most famous and prolific distributor of plan books was Sears, Roebuck and Company. Being thoroughly experienced in the catalog business by the time the bungalow boom came along, Sears began to offer not only the plans but also the materials to build a house by mail order as early as 1909. Through the engineering miracle of precut lumber that was carefully labeled for assembly, many houses were erected by do-it-yourself owners with a few helpers as well as by locally hired contractors. This mail-order phenomenon would have much to do with the bungalow's appearance in all parts of the country, far from any tract development that produced many such houses. Another retail giant, Montgomery Ward, also offered house plans in the same way, but on a somewhat smaller scale. Many other smaller firms followed their lead. Both of these companies had offices and sales people set up at outlets in virtually every major metropolitan area, smoothing the home-building process by providing personal assistance for the confused or wary customer. Financial assistance was also available from these outlets, and any serious (and employed) potential buyer would probably have had few obstacles in working out a deal for both the house and mortgage. Newlyweds and first-time buyers formed a good percentage of business for such package deals, which also offered habitual renters the opportunity to afford their own houses.

The most compelling reason for the success of such homes was their good value. For instance, a two-bedroom bungalow could be purchased from Sears's 1926 *Catalog of Homes* for only $629. At the other end of the spectrum was a four-bedroom, two-story Colonial Revival-style home with a formal dining room, den, and sun porch, which was offered in the same catalog for $4,909. This higher-priced model included a lot more than just a building "shell," for it included such itemized features as hardwood floors, a built-in breakfast nook, kitchen cabinets, and a dining-room china cabinet, as well as a built-in porch and hall seats. Although roofing materials and exterior paint were also part of the same package, certain essentials like the foundation, windows, electrical wiring, and interior plastering were subject to additional (though reasonable) charges. Another essential, the house lot, wasn't included either, but most lots were affordable through financing if they had not already been purchased. The mail-order bungalow business worked, and Sears alone had sold over 100,000 such homes by the mid-1930s. The Great

Depression, however, put a crimp in the business for the major manufacturers who were mostly hurt by losses on foreclosed properties they had financed.

Because of the availability today of a number of reprinted plan books from the period of the bungalow's greatest popularity, it is an amusing pastime to go scouting for favorite catalog homes, and the excitement of recognizing one is reward enough for the time spent in looking. In the Los Angeles area, which is considered the cradle of the bungalow style, huge tracts were subject to bungalow development and built within a few years of each other. Many still survive, remarkably intact. There were a number of plan-book companies that thrived on the rapid development of Los Angeles, and one such company is believed to have been responsible for selling almost 40,000 precut bungalows over a thirty-year period. While examples abound throughout the country, California led the way in promoting the popularity of the bungalow through its many publicized examples. While the Northern California cities of Oakland, Berkeley, and San Jose have the highest concentration of them in that part of the state, any city in America that experienced rapid growth in the early-twentieth century will invariably yield some fine examples, if not entire neighborhoods, of bungalows (figs. 17, 18).

Southern California provides an extraordinarily rich resource of bungalows that cannot be surpassed for variety and quality, both in contractor-built and custom-architect-designed homes. The salubrious climate and rocky terrain allowed great freedom of choice in materials and floor-plans. From the eastern reaches of the Los Angeles basin, west to the Pacific Ocean and south to San Diego, every community had its developments of familiar bungalow architecture. The area was in the midst of a real-estate boom in the early-twentieth century, and its prosperity can be traced in the waves of various popular housing styles that march across its landscape. Pasadena in particular, and its immediate environs of Glendale, Altadena, Sierra Madre, Monrovia, and Alhambra, provide some stellar examples for the bungalow watcher. Examples from the most modest to the most extravagant line the streets. This was the "land of the bungalow," as the title of the promotional song written in the 1920s proclaimed with confidence. The subject also inspired its share of "poetry," the most often-quoted example being the tongue-in-cheek *Bungal-Ode* by Burges Johnson, which was published by *Good Housekeeping* magazine in 1909. With any luck, there must be other similar masterpieces of kitsch waiting to be rediscovered and enjoyed again in a new context.

The business opportunities created by the bungalow craze were enough to spin the head of any budding businessman. Armed with an array of plan books, almost any enterprising person who had a penchant for selling things could probably have made a good living selling bungalows in their heyday, and many did. During the early decades of the twentieth century, developers and builders could promote tracts of land for bungalow development not only in California, but across the country, and have the tools to do it with very little investment except, of course, for the land. Florida was another center of land-boom fever that also embraced the bungalow for many of the same reasons as

5. The inglenook in the Howell (Doolittle) house in Altadena, California. Directly adjacent to a large living room, this fireplace alcove with built-in seating and bookcases creates an inglenook. This 1912 example is unusually large, and the door to the right of the fireplace provides access to other rooms. Most inglenooks are more compact than this one, and are generally created by having built-in seating next to a fireplace.

16

6. A living room. In 1921, the Morgan Woodwork Company of Oshkosh, Wisconsin, published a voluminous plan book called *Building with Assurance*, which featured bungalows as well as other houses. Short articles about home planning and decorating, accompanied by stylish renderings of finished interiors, promoted the armchair process of selecting and furnishing a home by catalog. Well integrated into this room's overall design by careful alignment with the ceiling beams, the fireplace area suggests an inglenook with its corner of built-in seating.

7. Design for an inglenook. This design made for the Morgan Woodwork Company emphasizes the cozy separateness of the fireplace ensemble from the rest of the adjacent living room. This inglenook has a lower ceiling height, and it is lit by wall sconces on either side of the decorative brick panel above the fireplace. Linked by a chair-rail molding, the high backs of the built-in benches align with the mantel shelf.

California had, and was much closer to the major population centers of the East Coast. Florida became one of the most successful tract-house venues in America, and it was comparable to the tract-house phenomenon that proliferated after World War II. In both cases, it was a matter of suppliers simply running to keep up with the demand.

The mania for plan books was active from just before 1910 and then on through the Twenties. With the increasing demand for bungalow plans, many rushed in to fill the need. Apparently, there were more than enough capable draftsmen available to adapt the latest tempting convenience or feature that might have been recently published in a magazine. The rustically detailed Craftsman-style bungalows were the most popular at first, and although they continued to appear in plan books well into the twenties, their heyday was closer to the period of World War I. The Orientalism that is usually seen in variations of the Craftsman style enjoyed a minor vogue, but could only draw on a limited range of effects that were definitively Oriental, such as the pagoda-like upswept gable peaks

8. Designs for a living room and a library. The successful use of color in harmony with the natural materials seen in the furniture, textiles, built-ins, and other woodwork, was a hallmark of bungalow interiors. The palettes of these two rooms illustrate how warm, neutralized colors of medium value are most compatible with the dark, natural woodwork. No matter what the color scheme, a gradual blending of dark to light values, rather than an abrupt contrast between wood and wall color, was always desirable. Both ceilings are painted a lighter tint of the wall color, another softening device far preferable to a stark white. These rooms appeared in a 1912 book called *Home Building and Decoration* by Henry Collins Brown.

seen on many Craftsman-style houses (figs. 1, 2). Another influence that could be successfully fused with the Craftsman style was that of the Swiss Chalet. The term *Japo-Swiss* was coined at the time to describe the unlikely union of influences from both Japan and Switzerland. The Swiss tradition of wooden cut-out forms on railings and prominent front-facing gables translated well to a Craftsman-style house. The Prairie style was most current for the bungalow market in the Teens, and although less popular in California than the Midwest, its rather modern appearance gave such homes greater longevity.

Fashion is always fickle, and various bungalow styles would evolve along with the gamut of popular taste. By the 1920s the demand for novelty historical-revival designs was paramount (fig. 15). Promoted by the Hollywood make-believe that the motion-picture industry fostered, the more progressive or modern house designs such as Craftsman or Prairie weren't shown in movies as much as the more familiar historic styles. By the Twenties the historic-period influences most in demand were the English, Spanish, and Colonial Revival styles. One Oakland, California, plan-book company solved the matter of making the right choice by offering the exact same floorplan combined with any one of those three styles for the exterior, and the variations were surprisingly successful (figs. 21, 22, 23). The Colonial Revival style in architecture had been strong in America since before the turn of the century, and this style has always had an ongoing appeal for furnishings as well as entire houses. Many houses that were built in another style altogether could usually accommodate some Colonial Revival furniture, and it was quite successfully included in Craftsman-style interiors. The Colonial Revival style continued in popularity well past the prime years of the bungalow, and in many places on the East Coast, especially, it has never disappeared. Variations on English and Spanish styles have also enjoyed long-term popularity, but on a lesser scale than American Colonial Revival.

The convenience and availability of numerous plan catalogs made it easy for the companies to reach their market, at the same time tempting the prospective homeowner to save money by doing some of the legwork and securing a buildable lot. Driven by the attractive economics of the deal, a large "do-it-yourself" market was attracted by the idea of constructing or finishing their own bungalows. Most design periodicals catered to this fact. Gustav Stickley, who published his houseplans for sale separately from his magazine, *The Craftsman*, gave strong support to budding homebuilders by showing them how to outfit and decorate the completed house properly. The angle of economy is always a critical one in business, and from this important point of view bungalows were one of the best deals going.

# Living in the Bungalow

## FEATURES OF PLANNING AND DESIGN

Regardless of the diversity of styles, forms, and detailing presented by the exteriors of bungalows, there are many common features that can be found in their planning and design. Most characteristic is the front porch that forms a transition from the outside to the inside, expressing important design elements of the exterior while helping to connect the house visually to its site. The porch is usually the focal point of the façade, part of an unfolding sequence of spaces leading from the street to the front door that establishes the character of the house. In some examples, the roofline of the porch has been extended over a side driveway to form a "porte cochère" or covered access from car to house, thus expanding the apparent size of the building (fig. 16). The use of strategically placed vegetation forges an important link between the house and the garden, and features such as planting urns, trellises, and windowboxes are common. Sometimes the front porch is completely open to the sky, with perhaps only a railing and partial overhang at the front door to define it. Some porch roofs are formed by open, pergola-like structures that accommodate climbing vines, and also allow more daylight to be admitted through otherwise shaded windows (figs. 58, 59). The notion of the porch as a flexible living area was promoted in the bungalow's heyday, and there is usually enough floor space to allow it to function as the touted outdoor living room (title page; figs. 3, 147). To be furnished appropriately, a porch swing was often included, perhaps along with woven wicker or rustic wooden Adirondack-style furniture, supplemented by lots of cushions, blankets, and a scattering of rugs. More than just a place of access to the house, the front porch forms a window on the world, whether it is a passing street scene, or the privacy of a garden vista. It can also imply the feeling of being a buffer against the outside world, yet at the same time allow direct communication with it. In bungalow developments extra wide or corner lots provided a good opportunity for wraparound or even multiple porches, which also help to make modestly scaled houses appear larger (figs. 14, 174).

The horizontality of bungalow design is reinforced by the shadow line of its porch, and the result is a greater dramatic emphasis given to the building's form and volume. Even with a porch of symmetrical design, it is quite typical to see a deliberately informal, asymmetrical placement of the front door and windows. Front porches in effect also function as outdoor entry halls, since the front doors of most bungalows open directly into their living rooms (figs. 6, 37). This familiar feature provides a casual sense of welcome to the visitor, and also facilitates the easy circulation of both air and people. Despite its compact scale, even

9. Design for a dining room. The wall divisions of a high wainscot surmounted by a plate rail and a broad frieze area are typical of most bungalow dining rooms. The wainscot panels are embellished with painted finishes, including a stenciled Art Nouveau-style frieze design, and a blended effect of sponging different colors together, known as a Tiffany finish. The leaded-glass windows and potted plants provide a link with nature, and a coordinated use of textiles is seen in the carpet, portière, curtains, and table scarf. This room design was specifically created to show how a wide variety of painted-finish effects could replace the need for wallpaper, evidence of the fierce competition between paint and wallpaper manufacturers for the home-decorating business. Compiled and published in 1910 by the Sherwin-Williams Paint Company's Decorative Department, the design is from *Your Home and its Decoration.*

10. (*Opposite*) Designs for a living room and dining room. These illustrations were included in Henry Collins Brown's 1912 book, *Home Building and Decoration,* and had previously been published in the 1910 catalog, *Handcraft Furniture,* by L. and J. G. Stickley. The living-room scheme uses a narrow green landscape frieze to suggest a touch of nature indoors. A copper fireplace hood inspired the reddish wall color, which harmonizes with the woodwork and furniture finish. The green of the frieze is repeated in the adjacent Morris chair, settle, and library table's leather top. The cool blue-gray tile facing of the fireplace provides an additional counterpoint. The dining-room scheme uses a matching grayish-green wood stain on both the furniture and woodwork, set off by the warm contrast of color seen in the high wainscot and carpet border. The wide frieze area is painted stucco, which forms a soft transition to an even paler ceiling.

11. Design for a kitchen. Much time was spent by housewives in bungalow kitchens, for servants were less likely to be found in the average middle-class home after the turn of the century. It was important that kitchens should be as bright, cheerful, and efficient as possible, and incorporate all the latest conveniences. Note in this kitchen design the durable tile wainscot and porcelain sink. A variation on the work-triangle plan favored in kitchen design is formed by the stove, the sink, and the wall cupboard at the right incorporating a work space. Wall lights flanking the sink illuminate the different heights of the built-in storage units. Illustrated in the 1921 plan book, *Building with Assurance* by the Morgan Woodwork Company, this kitchen has been drawn to look invitingly spacious.

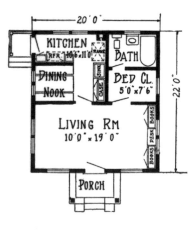

12. A compact bungalow design and floor plan. If necessary, even a small house could be further reduced to the absolute minimum. This example, which measures only twenty feet wide by twenty-two feet deep, was described as a "bungalowette" in the 1923 version of an annual publication by *Woman's Weekly* called *The Home.* The living room takes up almost half the floorspace of the entire house, and it features space-saving built-ins. One of the high-backed benches of the "dining nook" has been enlarged to accommodate a refrigerator and other storage on the back. The so-called "bed closet" on the plan appears too small to hold a folding Murphy bed. The tiny front porch and arched trellises help visually to enlarge the house.

13. Design of a sun porch. Often finding its way into other rooms of the bungalow, the use of wicker lounge furniture, complemented by colorful cushions, was a favorite choice for casual retreats. Published in the 1923 edition of *The Home*, this illustration was titled "In the Sun Parlor," and it could also easily serve as a guest room. The colors and patterns of the textiles illustrated here are evocative of the Art Deco style.

large gatherings may still be contained under one roof by using the porch as auxilliary entertainment space. Contributing to their enduring appeal is the floorplan flexibility built into most bungalows, such as extra doors connecting various rooms, or those leading to the porch or garden from the main living areas. Often, a small den or library is adjacent to the main living areas, lending further flexibility as a small home office or extra guest room (figs. 67, 175). Bungalow ceiling heights were considerably lower than their Victorian counterparts, contributing to the horizontal emphasis established by the design of the exterior.

A planning feature that characterizes most bungalow interiors dictates that living and dining rooms are open to each other, with the two spaces minimally divided. A typical arrangement has a broad opening cased in wood, with extra support provided on either side by two short, squared columns mounted on low walls, which may also contain built-in storage cabinets or bookcases (figs. 137, 156). This open-planning approach allows for longer vistas between the adjacent rooms, making the combined feeling of space greater than might otherwise be possible or expected for a modestly scaled house. Built-ins, an important element in bungalow interiors, reinforce this openness by supplanting the need for a lot of additional furniture. Windowseats and hall benches are particularly useful touches, providing

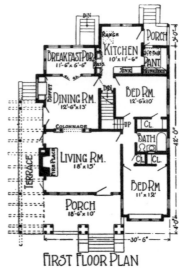
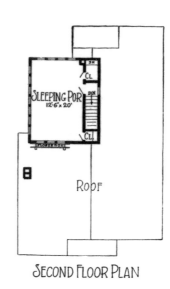

FIRST FLOOR PLAN          SECOND FLOOR PLAN

14. Design and plan of an "airplane bungalow." This type of house, so named for the "cockpit" feature of an attic room projecting above the "wings" of its roof, reflects a popular fascination with the concept of air travel. Published in *The Home* of 1923, the floor plan accommodates access to its upper level by means of an enclosed staircase between the dining room and an adjacent bedroom. Rather than make major design elements of them, most bungalows with direct access to their attics placed stairways in similarly discreet locations. This plan also features a raised, pergola-covered terrace along its left side, which extends the front-porch area, with additional access to the living and dining rooms. (For other examples of airplane bungalows, see figures 36 and 42.)

extra storage inside, as well as handy supplemental seating (figs. 49, 66, 137). There was at least one built-in bookcase in virtually every bungalow, and sometimes a compact drop-front desk was also incorporated into the design (fig. 176). The focal point of the main living area is invariably the fireplace, usually located for maximum visibility and impact, and forming a kind of altar to the cult of hearth and home that is fancifully associated with bungalow living. An architectural feature called an inglenook, featuring built-in seating adjacent to the fireplace in its own recessed alcove, almost forms a room-within-a-room (figs. 5, 7, 126). This feature is directly derived from the English Arts and Crafts style, and has historic precedent in otherwise unheated medieval stone manor houses, as a warm place to sit by the fire. Since space didn't usually permit this indulgence in the average bungalow, it was often implied by built-in benches on either side of a fireplace (fig. 164).

Another frequently seen detail is a pair of small windows, set high on the wall, flanking the fireplace. This was a popular location for using art-glass panels, colored and leaded, with either Prairie-style geometric designs, or other stylized floral forms and sometimes landscape scenes (fig. 170). A carry-over from the Victorian era, art-glass panels had a variety of applications elsewhere, including windows in front doors and their sidelights (figs. 125, 169), other doors (figs. 160, 175), narrow fixed panels above otherwise conventional windows (fig. 177), and as embellish-

ments to glass-fronted bookcases, built-in dining-room sideboards, and china cabinets (figs. 165,173,177).

Sometimes wide pocket doors are used to divide the living and dining rooms, inviting the pleasing effect of fabric panels, called portières, to be hung in these doorways (fig. 171). This was common practice at the time most bungalows were built, and avidly promoted by Gustav Stickley and other tastemakers, who recommended embroidery and appliqué work on fabric as a suitable way of integrating handicraft into the interior. Most old houses will reveal, upon close inspection, evidence of there having been portière hardware in the doorways. Not only were the portières decorative, but they also served to block drafts, buffer noise, and conserve heat, and often repeated the design of adjacent window draperies. Other popular textiles of the period were pillows and table scarves (figs. 176, 187), which could showcase the craft skills of an occupant, and were popularly exchanged as gifts. Such household needlework projects, commonly sold in "kit" form, catered to the do-it-yourself mindset of the bungalow culture and are currently enjoying a welcome revival.

Generally speaking, the warmth of natural woodwork was considered appropriate in the main living areas. Typical features like box-beamed ceilings, door and window casings, and various built-ins showcased the pleasing color and textural variations of wood (figs. 37–40). Types of wood varied, of course, by geographic location and budget, with fir being the most common; oak, cedar, chestnut,

15. Frontispiece of *The Home,* 1923. This bright, enticing image of an idealized home was created for *Woman's Weekly,* who sent this annual publication of homemaking advice and design ideas only to their subscribers. This Chicago periodical also included legal advice about borrowing money and buying houses. This depiction of a cozy English-style cottage in a garden setting obviously had a strong appeal in the twenties (and would not be sneered at today).

mahogany, or gumwood were more costly and therefore less typical in modest houses. California's convenient supply of redwood made it an early and popular choice as a finish material there, but its rising cost and limited range of staining options led to the greater use of other wood such as fir by the late teens and twenties. Hardwood floors were favored as being easy to maintain, and were considered less likely to harbor dust and germs than the wall-to-wall carpeting favored in the Victorian era. An almost obsessive awareness of things believed to be healthful also included the importance of fresh air through good ventilation, which was reflected in the open planning of bungalows, and in the multiple door and window configurations providing cross-drafts. Wood floors, sometimes embellished with decorative border insets of different colored woods, provided an effective backdrop for the popular use of Oriental or American Indian-style rugs (figs. 37, 66, 88).

Wood paneling was frequently carried up the walls to form a high wainscot and usually capped by a plate rail, which was a shallow, grooved shelf for the display of plates, trays, pottery, small pictures, or other objects (figs. 38, 157, 172). A plate rail was almost always found in the dining room, but it was also occasionally carried throughout the

main living and circulation spaces in some houses. When wood upgrades were desirable but not affordable, a viable option was the use of painted graining on a less expensive wood. The creation of various facsimiles of more expensive woods had been a popular solution to the same problem throughout the nineteenth century, and virtually every experienced housepainter was skilled in rendering *faux bois* (painted graining) and other types of decorative painting (fig. 173). The art of painted finishes is enjoying a major revival today, and in addition to graining, other finishes for walls like sponging and glazing are appropriate and effective ways to use color in the interior of a bungalow, and they also have historic precedent.

A particularly useful and effective supplement to overall painted finishes is the use of stenciling, usually found as a decorative border or frieze above a high wooden wainscot or a picture molding of a corresponding height (figs. 169, 171, 172). The height of this frieze area could vary, but somewhere between eighteen and twenty-four inches was most typical. Preferred motifs included stylized plant forms as pleasing contrasts to the linearity of the woodwork, or tailored geometrics that underscored the architecture. Sometimes the ceiling panels or coffers created by

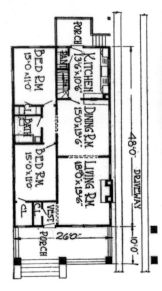

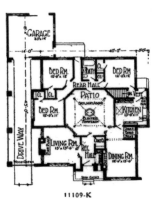

16. Two bungalows and their plans (A Craftsman-style above, and a Spanish Colonial Revival-style below). These 1923 offerings from *The Home* exhibit some popular features of bungalow design, such as the pergola-covered porte-cochère. This spans an adjacent driveway in the Craftsman example, linking it to the landscape and helping to make a narrow house look wider. The Spanish example has a patio plan, with a fountain in the center. Inspired by the courtyards of early California haciendas, the patio plan also allows for outdoor circulation and direct access to all areas of the house. The small, walled forecourt and gated driveway help visually to expand the house. Although less popular in colder climates, where the patio space might have been covered and skylighted, various forms of Spanish and Mission-derived styles occurred across the country.

box-beam ceilings were further embellished by stenciled or handpainted borders (fig. 130). Stenciling was another convenient and appropriate vehicle for handicraft in the bungalow interior.

With their typical preponderance of dark woodwork, color schemes of these early-twentieth century interiors favored earthy and pleasingly neutralized shades of sand, golden ochre, yellow- or blue-green, deep teal, soft red, or warm terra cotta in the main living spaces. Walls were often painted one color, with another color or perhaps a repeating pattern used to define the frieze area (figs. 10, 37). Today's common insistence on "light-and-airy" rooms, and especially the conspicuous lack of color that predominates most contemporary interiors, was not considered appropriate for the main living spaces of most bungalows that were used for family gatherings and entertainment. Paler, softer color schemes did exist, but they were typically reserved for bedrooms (figs. 182, 197). It was, in fact, quite usual in these private areas for the woodwork to be painted in pale shades or even white. In contrast, to

envelop the guest with a warm, cozy, and welcoming feeling upon entry into the bungalow was a primary goal that was preached in nearly every design-advice book and periodical of the day. The use of colors in harmony with natural wood tones, not in stark contrast to them, was the obvious and preferred way to accomplish this. Sometimes the color scheme of a bungalow interior was solely the rich hues of natural wood, used on occasion for all of a room's wall and ceiling surfaces. In such interiors, additional interest might be introduced through a raised or peaked ceiling, perhaps further enhanced with beams and appropriate lighting fixtures (fig. 49). Such rooms are less typical, but they epitomize the atmosphere of an ideal bungalow interior, and need little further embellishment.

Another convenient and popular way to introduce color into the interior was with wallcoverings, offering many options of texture and pattern. A restrained yet effective choice was the appealingly rough texture of a simple burlap fabric or perhaps even a grasscloth, in a harmonious color, that was used on walls and sometimes on ceilings in

17. Wild Rose Avenue, Monrovia, California. While the same bungalow styles occur throughout America, this streetscape is particularly characteristic of many in Southern California. This neighborhood was developed about the time of World War I, and many of its homes are in the prevailing Craftsman style. An exception in this block is the house (second from the left) that shows a distinctly Colonial Revival influence in its paired white classical columns.

18. Sterling Avenue, Alameda, California. This architecturally diverse Northern California island community, adjacent to Oakland, has a number of bungalow enclaves, but it is best known for its wonderful Victorian homes. This pastel-hued procession of houses was developed as a tract in the twenties. No matter where they may be located, the term *California Bungalow* is sometimes used to describe similar small houses, usually with stucco façades and simplified Craftsman-style detailing. An individual identity for each house is achieved by the varying shapes of the porch columns.

lieu of paint (figs. 88, 89, 170). If the material wasn't a woven fabric, it was probably a paper that was embossed and printed to resemble cloth. Occasionally seen are metallic gold-bronze finishes on these fabric-like textures, handsome for their richly reflective effects between wooden ceiling beams (figs. 142, 144, 146). Wallcoverings that simulated even more elegant materials, such as woven tapestries, were favored for use in dining rooms as friezes above the typical high wainscot. Other effects, such as the simulation of embossed and tooled leather, were also desirable as friezes, and some were manufactured with their finish already applied and ready to hang (fig. 177). An alternative choice to this effect could be achieved by applying paint in an appropriate technique to an unfinished, durable wallcovering such as Anaglypta, a heavy embossed paper, or Lincrusta, a paper-backed, linoleum-like material that was more deeply embossed. These materials could be painted to resemble a number of other materials, including wood, metal, and plasterwork. Both of these materials have survived since the nineteenth century because of their economy and adaptability to any color scheme through their many finishing options. Manufactured as narrow borders, friezes, dadoes (or wainscots), and overall patterns for walls and ceilings, they remain a viable and available choice today (figs. 173, 184).

In addition to the wallcoverings already mentioned, the use of conventional wallpapers has always had a widespread appeal, and its applications in the bungalow interior were many. Generally speaking, wallpaper delivered a lot of impact for its cost, which if machine-printed, usually was quite reasonable. Wide friezes were made with coordinating narrow borders and overall wall-fill patterns, forming convenient sets that lent themselves to various types of application (figs. 165, 175, 176, 186, 187). Wallpaper designs available to the average bungalow owner comprised a vast range of machine-printed goods, with some reflecting the various influences also seen in bungalow architecture such as the Craftsman, Prairie, and Colonial Revival styles. Probably most common were large-scale florals with matching borders that were considered most appropriate for bedrooms. There were many variations on leafy patterns that were loosely inspired by the work of William Morris, as well as many simple stripes and especially the overall fabric-like textures mentioned above. Hand-printed Morris papers, which are still obtainable, were usually too expensive for the average bungalow owner (figs. 74, 185, 186). Ceiling papers continued to be produced as part of coordinating wallpaper sets as they had been in the Victorian era, but they were scaled down for use, if used at all, in much simpler designs appropriate to lower ceilings. The use of a mica pigment, with its light-reflecting qualities, did continue to be used in some wall and ceiling papers. Among the more progressive designs

were geometric pendant-style friezes with a distinctive Prairie-style influence, which was the most modern look available in the Teens and Twenties. Pendant friezes are characterized by their distinctive repeating pattern, featuring a stylized design element that appears to be hanging or suspended from the rest of the frieze at rhythmic intervals, hence the term *pendant*. Another wallpaper treatment with an almost architectural approach that enjoyed great popularity was the concept of wall panelization, achieved by using narrow paper borders as moldings to create rectilinear frames or panels containing an overall wallpaper pattern or texture. Another variation combined narrow borders below a matching frieze, thus dividing the available wall area into a series of narrow vertical panels similar in proportion to board-and batten-style wood wainscoting. These kinds of paper treatments offered a much less expensive and more easily changed alternative to wooden millwork used to create the same kind of wall divisions.

What sets bungalow planning apart from that of most other small houses is the almost obsessive attention to practicality that distinguishes it. The kitchen, traditionally the heart of the home, was reduced in size from its Victorian predecessor to save steps and energy, as well as space. Early practical innovations included the California Cooler, a food-storage cabinet that was vented directly to the outside air from its location in the wall of the kitchen or utility porch, perhaps so named because of its popularity in the mild Golden State. Compact eating areas, described as breakfast nooks, were directly adjacent to the kitchen and allowed families a secondary mealtime gathering place that also saved time, steps, and maintenance for the housewife. This compulsion for convenience also reflected, after the turn of the century, the move away from the use of domestic servants by the average middle-class household, and it was only the larger and grander versions of the bungalow that had maid's rooms adjacent to their kitchens. Breakfast nooks were typically furnished with high-backed, built-in benches that usually faced each other, with a fixed or sometimes folding table surface set between them. In the smallest bungalows, such eating areas entirely replaced any other dining room (fig. 12).

The advent of new kitchen technology in the early-twentieth century coincided with the popularity of the bungalow, and introduced new cooking stoves that used gas from city utilities instead of coal (figs. 11, 90). Familiar conveniences of today like electric refrigeration were in the process of being perfected and didn't become commonplace until the later twenties. By that time, the typical middle-class kitchen might well have contained a rather wide array of electric time-savers such as toasters, mixers, waffle irons, fans, water kettles, and perhaps even an early version of the dishwater. The washboard and washtub that

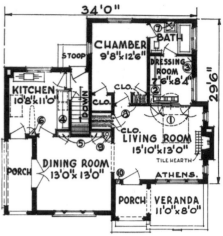

19. Spanish Colonial Revival bungalow and plan. Illustrated in *Loizeaux's Plan Book No. 7*, published in 1927, this house shows the continuing interest in Spanish-derived styles that peaked in the Twenties. The towered entry porch, adjacent verandah, and canvas awnings give the building a street presence that belies its size. To supplement the single bedroom (called "chamber" on the plan), the use of a folding Murphy bed is indicated in the living room. The descriptive copy states that "the living room becomes an airy bedroom at night," suggesting that this was highly desirable.

might still be on the utility porch were soon to be replaced by cylindrical electric washing machines with protruding ringers. Built-in ironing boards and electric irons were already a commonplace feature. Then, as now, Americans were fascinated and intrigued by the prospect of how modern technology could improve their lives, and the bungalow became a kind of proving ground for many conveniences that we associate with modern living.

Bathrooms, to a large extent, were carryovers from their late-Victorian counterparts, especially early in this century. The basic conveniences of indoor toilets, hot and cold running water, and the choices of a soak in the bathtub or a quick shower were already well established in the American middle-class home before the turn of the century. The outward appearance of the bathroom was slow to change, and like the kitchen favored easily cleaned surfaces. A typical bathroom wall surface was ceramic tile, usually being white rectangular tiles that were laid horizontally to form a wainscot of about half the height of the wall (fig. 41). The flooring most often seen with this type of wall treatment consists of small hexagonal tiles that were of a harder and more durable porcelain material than the glazed ceramic tiles on the walls. Similar tiled wall treatments might be seen in kitchens, especially around the sink and stove, but flooring there was generally a sheet of patterned linoleum laid over a soft wood subflooring,

which might be painted in enamel or even grained where it was exposed around the room's perimeter. Sometimes hardwood floors of oak or maple were used in the kitchens of more expensive houses. Built-in cabinets were typical in most bungalow kitchens to maximize space, and sometimes ran floor-to-ceiling on one or more walls (fig. 40). If built-ins were minimal or inadequate, storage needs were sometimes supplemented by a "Hoosier" cabinet—a kitchen standby for years that is a free-standing piece of furniture with storage bins and cupboards for food, supplies, and utensils. Built-in cabinet styles were certainly plain if not severe, with the possible use of clear glass-fronted cabinets used above lower counter-height cabinets if space and budget permitted. In the average-size bungalow kitchens were engineered with the compactness of a ship, and few were able to accommodate much open space as many kitchens do today. They were essentially utility areas, and outside of the linoleum pattern or perhaps the area of the breakfast nook itself, decoration was minimal. Sometimes a simple stenciled or paper border might find its way into the kitchen (fig. 11). There was also popular use of "sanitary" wallpapers, so-called because of their washability. With an applied varnished surface, these were considered appropriate for kitchens and bathrooms, and their designs were usually intended to resemble ceramic-tile patterns. While it is exceedingly rare for an original kitchen or bathroom wallcovering to have survived, they (and other popular wallpapers of the period) are well documented in surviving pattern books. In the utility areas, good natural light was an important consideration. This was an era when electric light was still in its fledgling stages, and many of the earlier bungalows were actually built with both gas and electric light. In bathrooms, the combination of two small operable windows flanking a mirrored medicine cabinet is relatively common, and sometimes more extensive built-in arrangements for linens and toiletries are also seen (fig. 41). Toward the end of the Twenties, colored ceramic tiles began to be seen in bathrooms and kitchens, sometimes simply as an accent band with mostly white tiles still predominating. Soon, wide availability of colored fixtures as well as tiles would redefine the appearances of bathrooms, and by the later thirties, new kitchens were becoming even more streamlined, along with appliances and cars.

The idea of locating most, if not all, of the bathrooms on the same level as the main living areas is additional evidence of practicality in bungalow planning (figs. 2, 16, 19, 23). The main reason usually cited is that doing so saved steps and therefore energy, presumably thought to be better spent doing something more constructive than climbing up and down a lot of stairs. In the most successful bungalow plans, the bedrooms are distanced from the main living spaces as much as possible by the use of a connecting hallway that separates the two areas. Usually located off this hallway is the bathroom, often placed between two bedrooms, and sometimes having doors that connect it to either bedroom, as well as to the hall. This maximum sense of separation and privacy in such a com-

pact house has retained its usefulness and appeal for today's occupants.

An interesting aspect of bungalow planning was the way it seemed to take space away from the private and utilitarian parts of the house, and give it back to the main living areas. This was justified by the belief that the bedrooms and kitchen required only a minimum of space to function efficiently, thereby conserving more space to be incorporated into the main living areas, where it was felt to be more needed. Because of the compact size of the bedrooms, their storage capacity was sometimes supplemented by built-in drawer or shelving units located in or near the closet, thus lessening the need for more furniture to crowd the room. Mechanical folding-bed units, actually a nineteenth-century innovation, found new popularity in bungalows by providing additional flexibility to their floor plans. Sometimes called Murphy beds, these frequently appear in plan books and periodicals as a solution to the potential need for extra sleeping accommodations. Usually these folding beds were located to open into the living room or dining room from a deep closet. The unit, hinged to flip down for use, was secured to the back of its closet door, so that to use the bed the door was fully opened and the bed was lowered into place. For storage, it was flipped back up and secured so that the closet door could swing closed, and the bed unit disappeared from sight. Although some of these vintage folding-bed units have survived, most have been removed to expand the closet they once occupied.

There was another area of many bungalow interiors that could be utilized as extra sleeping space for guests, but this was not its primary purpose. This was the sleeping porch, a

20. Spanish Colonial Revival bungalow, Pasadena, California. Located in the Bungalow Heaven Landmark District, this well-tended house closely resembles the "Athens" model of Loizeaux's plan book (fig. 19), of which it is almost a mirror image. To address the varying requirements of certain site plans, reversing the component parts of a house was a usual option offered by plan-book companies. The canvas awning supported by arrow-tipped poles, is also close to what is shown in the plan book.

kind of vestigial legacy of the vacation house that forms part of the bungalow's ancestry. The essential point of the sleeping porch was that it enabled occupants to have the option of sleeping in the fresh air, unfettered by stuffiness or over-heating that was believed to impede a healthy, good night's sleep. If not part of the original construction plan, sleeping porches could be readily added on as simple "shed-roof" structures attached to the side of the house. Some bungalows were built with more than one sleeping porch, and over time many of these porches have been fully enclosed to become additional bedrooms. Even when they were first constructed, many sleeping porches were used more as sun porches or sun rooms, and thus outfitted with appropriate furnishings (figs. 13, 135). Usually there was some kind of daybed or sofa to allow for a possible guest visit or the occasional afternoon nap, along with assorted houseplants that were likely to thrive in such a light-filled space. Most sleeping porches were enclosed by rows of screen-fitted windows placed side-by-side. In colder climates, storm windows kept the worst of the winter at bay until the screens could be put back in place in the spring. Most sleeping porches were chiefly used during hot weather, providing a cooler place for sleeping at night. This is also how they were used in summer homes across the country, but in milder climates they could be used throughout the year. Attic-level spaces, usually accommodated under a generous dormer or a gable end, were another potential location for sleeping porches. A practical interior wall and ceiling finish for such a space was narrow, unpainted tongue-and-groove siding, which had proven appropriate in many vacation homes for its ease of maintenance and tidy appearance.

Another novel way that attic levels were incorporated into bungalow design is seen in a hybrid form known as the "airplane bungalow" (figs. 14, 36, 42). In these homes, an attic-level room was designed to project above the peak of the main roofline, making such a room similar to the raised cockpit of an early twentieth-century airplane. Set above the broad sweep of the bungalow's roofline, comparable to an airplane's wings, this upper room was often first built as a screened-in sleeping porch. Later, many such spaces were enclosed to create a playroom, extra bedroom space, or a retreat. Its desirability was enhanced by the fact that it was likely to have the best view in the house, as well as the ability to catch cooling breezes from its lofty height.

In addition to the potential of sleeping-porch locations, the undeveloped attic space of the typical bungalow was another one of its selling points. To prospective buyers who often had growing families, there was an obvious appeal in the possibility of future expansion into the space enclosed by the all-embracing roof. In terms of outward appearances, an attic level converted to active use would not necessarily be perceptible from the outside, so the

original integrity of the building's roofline was likely to be preserved intact.

Although more could be discussed about the furniture, lighting, and interior design that is typical of the bungalow style, the photographs and captions that follow will provide much more information about those subjects. The purpose of this book is to illustrate and discuss the bungalow in all its variety as America's Arts and Crafts home.

# Preserving the Bungalow
## ITS FATE IN THE FUTURE

In recent years, there has been a groundswell of interest in recognizing that the bungalow, as a significant and historic type of American housing, should be preserved. This movement has been steadily building, and there is good reason to believe that it will continue. Interest in the bungalow has been given much of its momentum by an ever-increasing public recognition and appreciation of the Arts and Crafts Movement, which has taken place over the past two decades. Historians, museum curators, and collectors are among the first to recognize and establish the historic and artistic significance of a period, and it was their interest and efforts that generated numerous museum exhibitions on the subject, and the diversity of related resource materials available today.

The first surge of rekindled interest across the country was expertly launched in 1972 by a traveling exhibition entitled "The Arts and Crafts Movement in America 1876–1916," organized by the Art Museum at Princeton University, and The Art Institute of Chicago. This exhibition was an opportunity for the general public to be exposed to the importance and beauty of the objects created during the Movement. The catalog for this landmark exhibition has become a standard reference work on the subject. Another important early exhibition that was devoted to a key part of the Movement was called "California Design 1910." Although on display at the Pasadena Center for only six weeks in late 1974, the exhibition proved to be of great significance in promoting further identification and knowledge of California's specific contributions to the American Arts and Crafts Movement. These exhibitions were splendid showcases of fine objects in the various categories of decorative arts, and they did much to educate the public about the important names, special skills, and signature styles of the finest craftspeople and most important workshops of the period.

Although the objects displayed took the limelight, both exhibitions also brought attention to the work of important architects of that time. The work of such architects as

PER/PECTIVE/ /HOWING THE COMPLETED BUILDING

21. Three perspective sketches of bungalow designs. Marketed in the Twenties by the W.W. Dixon Plan Service of Oakland, California, these designs appeared in *Dixon's Book of Working Drawings.* Each exterior was designed to be completely interchangeable with an identical floor plan (fig. 23). Once a customer had selected a suitable floorplan, they had the additional choice of either the Spanish (left), English (right), or Colonial (center) style for the exterior of their house. Ranging from three to six-room arrangements, each floor plan in the Dixon book was offered in these three different exterior styles.

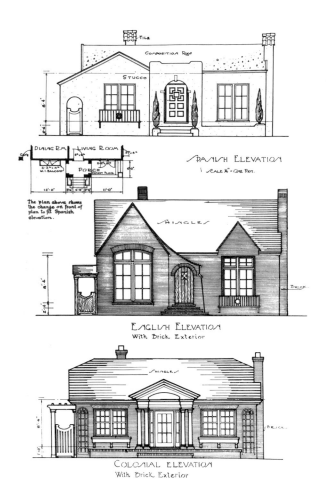

22. Elevations of three bungalow designs. The exteriors seen in the perspective sketches (fig. 21) are more clearly documented in these drawings. In light of the basic arrangement of the central front door that is flanked by two equal-width windows, there is a surprising degree of variety in each elevation. The English and Colonial designs, shown here with a brick facing, were also available in stucco versions. The Dixon book included the disclaimer that they were "not architects but publishers of stock plans."

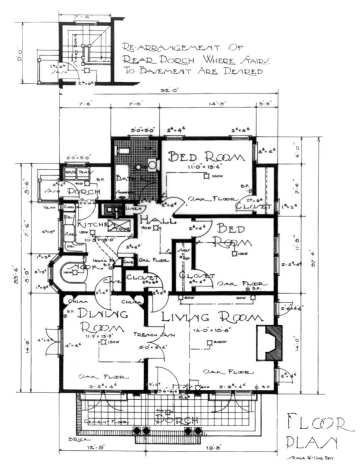

A FIVE ROOM COTTAGE.

23. Floor plan for "A Five-Room Cottage." This same plan was available from the W.W. Dixon Plan Company in the customer's choice of three different exterior styles (figs. 21, 22). The porch plan shown here includes the paired columns of the Colonial version. There was a conspicuous avoidance of the term *bungalow* in this plan book, despite the inclusion of many examples. Perhaps this company was already perceiving a shift away from the term's long popularity, which began to fade, especially after 1930, in favor of the ubiquitous *cottage* label.

24. Batchelder garage and guest house, Pasadena, California. This building was constructed in 1928 by famed Arts and Crafts tile-designer and manufacturer Ernest Batchelder (1875–1957) adjacent to his 1909 house in Pasadena (fig. 68). One of the most interesting features of the place are the large, hand-wrought-iron strap hinges on the weathered wood of the folding garage doors. For increased ventilation, there are insets of pierced and glazed ceramic tiles in the doors and gable peak of the garage. The scale and basic concept of this building makes an interesting comparison to that of the so-called "garlow" (fig. 25).

Greene and Greene (Charles Sumner Greene, 1868–1957, and his brother Henry Mather Greene, 1870–1954), Irving Gill (1870–1936), Bernard Maybeck (1862–1957), and Louis Christian Mullgardt (1866–1942), to name a few, brought the architectural achievements of the Arts and Crafts Movement into focus. Their finest commissions were highlighted, and included among them were some significant smaller projects that were (or could have been) described as bungalows. This was an early indication that this type of building deserved further study. Although it is usually difficult to document or confirm, the work of the most prominent architects is that which is most likely to have influenced their lesser-known or anonymous colleagues through publication in books and periodicals. Since the vast majority of bungalows were not built by famous architects, and have been largely ignored, it is these houses that are most in need of recognition. It is through the spreading of public awareness of the bungalow's importance in American history that a strong impetus for its preservation can be created and sustained.

One barrier that has negatively affected preservation efforts for bungalows is the common perception that they aren't old enough to warrant much concern about preserving them. Another hurdle is that of having to overcome the general public apathy about the issue. Many would even deny a problem exists because there are still so many bungalows to be found throughout the country. Conversely, time is one factor that has worked in favor of bungalow preservation. As we rapidly approach the next century, many people no longer think that these houses aren't old enough to warrant serious consideration for preservation. Being almost a century old is coming true for many bungalows, thus convincing more of the public that they are indeed old. The question is: when does an old house become "historic?" After all, that seems to be the magic word that triggers people into action about preservation. A house apparently assumes the mantle of history when its period takes on a rosier glow through distance and perspective, and its image somehow becomes particularly emblematic or evocative of its era.

The present attitude toward bungalows and other Arts and Crafts houses compares to a similar situation of about twenty years ago, when the movement to preserve Victorian-era houses was still in its infancy. It wasn't very long before people across the country were rediscovering the beauty of Victorians, and the movement to preserve and restore them soon was well underway. The Victorian preservation movement continues and shows no sign of dwindling. This new appreciation of Victorians created a resurging demand for specialized restoration skills and products, as well as for the collectibles of the era. Looking back further, the same thing could be said about the revival of interest in the American Colonial era, an interest that has been continuing strongly since the nation's Centennial year of 1876 was celebrated by the great Exposition in Philadelphia. Every era of American history deserves attention and study, and it is an ongoing process that doesn't stop with fashion or generational changes, although these factors affect the revival forms that various styles assume. Old houses tell us something about ourselves as a

25. A "garlow" design and plan. The now-obscure term *garlow* combines the words "garage" and "bungalow." This design and plan was published in the 1923 version of *The Home*, along with three other examples in different styles. The "garlow" was intended to combine both automobile and living space, either on a temporary or permanent basis. In this example, by constructing a garage space to which separate living quarters were attached, more permanent uses were built in from the start. This arrangement could function as temporary owner housing, and could later be used as servant or rental housing after the main house was completed.

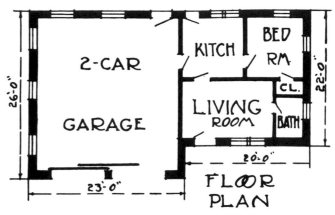

26. Site plan of St. Francis Court, Pasadena, California. Designed by Sylvanus Marston in 1909, this is one of the earliest-known examples of bungalow-court planning. First popularized as seasonal rental housing in the mild California climate, this court assembles a group of individual houses around a common garden space. The size of these units is more generous than those of the typical bungalow court. St. Francis Court was eventually replaced by a department store.

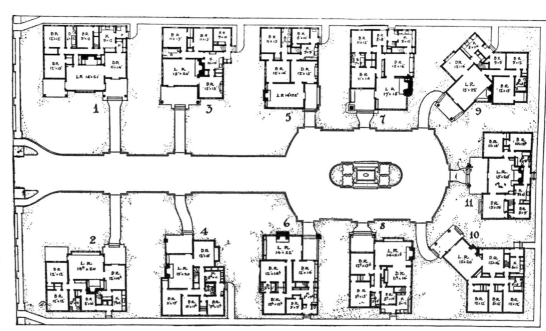

culture, and bungalows are as revealing as any about the period in which they were constructed. They tell us a true story about American culture in the early twentieth century, and the audience for it is steadily increasing.

It is a recurring observation that the end of a century is a logical time to reassess the accomplishments of the past, and perhaps even revive some good ideas that may have been prematurely discarded in the name of fashion or progress. It is also a time to shed outmoded ideas and implement new ones in the spirit of the new century. Since age is relative, the different generational associations with bungalows vary widely. Bungalows, after almost thirty years of being highly popular, fell out of fashion during the years of the Great Depression after 1930. The premises that had once made bungalows seem new and progressive were eventually considered outmoded. The very word "bungalow" became a victim of popular culture and took on a derogatory connotation. As usual, the younger generation wanted something new that they could claim as their own. The Modern Movement arrived conveniently enough for that, even if drastic changes in the world economy affected its progress at first. It wasn't long, however, before the need for greater economy and efficiency brought new technology and materials to the forefront of new housing. In the Thirties and Forties house forms did change outwardly, but most small-scale middle-class homes were an uninspired, watered-down pastiche of vaguely historical-revival styles. Modernism at its most progressive was still not part of most people's daily lives except through their automobiles and electric gadgetry. Most examples of modern domestic architecture, without overt historic references, occurred after World War II, although historicism has never entirely disappeared. It is a bit ironic that some of the planning ideas that were pioneered in bungalow design would actually be retained and reinterpreted in later tract-housing design under a slightly different guise, and called by a different name. For example, living and dining rooms that flow together, smallish bedrooms conveniently located on the same level, and patios or decks to accommodate outdoor entertaining are familiar bungalow derivatives that are all seen in the postwar ranch-style tract house. It is a direct descendant of the bungalow, and it is probable that some time in the future these houses will also be the object of a preservation movement.

Let us look at the efforts that have been successful in creating an awareness of bungalows, and establishing the momentum to preserve them. One particularly shining example is a Pasadena, California, neighborhood that is now officially known and recognized as the Bungalow Heaven Landmark District. A ten-square-block area of mostly modestly scaled, middle-class homes on pleasant, tree-shaded streets, it has the distinction of being that city's first (and so far, only) historic district. This gently sloping District, north of downtown Pasadena, was first annexed by the city in 1906, and most of the houses were built in the soon-to-follow years of "bungalow mania." True to its name, the neighborhood boasts an extraordinary variety of bungalow styles, shapes, and sizes (figs. 20, 46, 47, 56, 61). Although some blocks of the District are still in a transition stage, many homes have already been beautifully restored, inside and out.

The movement to preserve this area developed from a number of factors. Like so many urban neighborhoods across the country, the District experienced a gradual decline, starting in the postwar years. Some longtime residents, who had lived there since the beginning, died or had moved elsewhere. An increasing number of the houses became rental properties owned by absentee landlords, and some of them were divided into apartments. When some vintage bungalows were lost to high-density apartment complexes, completely out of scale and out of context with the neighborhood, a warning flag went up to many of its residents that something had to be done. With the higher density came increasing urban problems. Some residents fought back and eventually won by achieving "downzoning" of most of the area to single-family homes, with a few exceptions at the outer boundaries. Next came the interest in preserving the architectural character of the bungalows that remained, as another major problem was insensitive alterations, which were occurring at an alarming rate.

It was a major movement of neighborhood activism that led the city to consider a conservation plan to prohibit demolition and limit alterations that would affect the essential period character of the area. A crusade of signature-gathering volunteers, led by resident Robert Kneisel, set about to sell their idea of landmark-district status to each neighbor on a door-to-door basis. Two years later, their combined energy and perseverance had officially brought the issue before the City Council. It was through additional help by two sympathetic local groups, the Urban Conservation Office and Pasadena Heritage, that Bungalow Heaven finally received its official designation in 1989.

There is every indication that this has been a good development for the District. The first effect was a boost of the residents' morale, and a new awareness that the area was indeed special. Those who had been previously unaware of or indifferent to the significance of bungalows now had a better understanding of their homes and access to help on how to maintain them properly. Other nearby neighborhoods took notice and also gained from the benefit of observation and example. The area also became more desirable to prospective new residents, and there has been

27. Bungalow court, San Diego, California. Located in the city's North Park district, this court features simple Mission Revival houses and tidy landscaping, arranged around a central lawn. Similar developments sprang up along new streetcar-line extensions and catered to newly arrived working people. The tiny scale of these units was best suited for one or two persons. Featuring rear service access for ice and milk deliveries, the room layout of these units is very similar to that shown in figure 12.

28. The Reinway bungalow court, Pasadena, California. Surviving in a well-maintained condition, this complex was designed in 1916 by architects Buchanan and Brockway. The original owner and builder had living quarters in the two-story building visible at the far end of the court. The pergola-style entrance portal retains its original back-lit signage.

29. Typical street signage for the Bungalow Heaven Landmark District, Pasadena, California. The District was established in 1989, and it has encouraged an increasing awareness, revitalization, and historic preservation of bungalow neighborhoods across the country.

a corresponding gain in property values since the designation. Many of the houses benefited from appropriate period restoration and landscaping schemes.

The Bungalow Heaven Neighborhood Association has found that staging an annual house tour has been a convenient and successful way to raise funds for neighborhood improvements that aren't forthcoming from tightened city budgets. The house tours have generated funds for scholarships, playground equipment in centrally located McDonald Park, and a Park Watch safety program. Neighborhood clean-ups have been organized, and there has also been a decrease in crime and graffiti as a result of neighbors getting involved. Attractive Bungalow Heaven street signage, proclaiming the entrance points to the District, has been erected with house-tour profits (fig. 29). Signature items such as T-shirts, coffee mugs, posters, and note cards are sold for profit at the tours to help keep the ticket prices as low as possible. Raffles of related Arts and Crafts-style goods and services flourish with generous donations from local businesses.

Needless to say, the real driving force behind the success of this neighborhood's transformation is the volunteered time and energy of its residents. Every phase of what they have accomplished has been made possible by donations of relevant expertise and boundless enthusiasm. The house tour requires the most effort and coordination, but it has fostered the greatest tangible rewards to the neighborhood. Usually featuring about eight houses, each one is staffed by volunteer docents in each room. Promotion efforts for the event are well underway eight or nine months in advance of the tour, which has been found to work best in Pasadena during the milder temperatures of April rather than in the heat of the summer. A well-organized publicity campaign pursues local media coverage, and it now has a mailing list of over 700 publications, organizations, businesses, and individuals that are contacted. The most recent tour attracted over 2,300 people, who came from all over the country. The most important result of all of this is, of course, the thousands of people each year who are reminded of the important place that bungalows occupy in our culture and architectural history. These people, in turn, form many links to others not able to attend, but who are still able to learn by the all-important word of mouth.

Although the success of Bungalow Heaven is a classic example of continuous historic preservation, the movement to preserve bungalow neighborhoods across the country is growing and needs further recognition and support. For example, there are already similar associations in Florida, including the Old Seminole Heights National Register Historic District in Tampa, which has fought the widening of streets in their bungalow neighborhood. The Kenwood Neighborhood Association was formed in St. Petersburg in 1990, and because it has the highest concentration of bungalows in that city, it received a grant from the local government for a signage program. In Decatur, Georgia, there is the Great Lakes Neighborhood Association, which has helped preserve its mix of historic architecture, including bungalows, through local education efforts about sensitive and appropriate renovation. A Madison, Wisconsin, neighborhood recently earned its recognition as the Marquette Bungalow Historic District and is seeking additional recognition from the National Register. The Longfellow neighborhood of South Minneapolis, Minnesota, is forming a bungalow association. These examples are just the tip of the proverbial iceberg for the bungalow-preservation movement. Most communities have local historical societies already in place, which can be another vehicle for education and events to benefit awareness of bungalow districts or noteworthy individual houses. The process can be a creative, fun, and rewarding one. The main lesson to learn from this book is that bungalow architecture deserves to be treasured, so that future generations will have the same resources for delving into those aspects of American culture that are still here today.

We know, of course, that different versions of the bungalow are to be found throughout the world, but America has made the style its own. Bungalows are as much a part of our heritage as the corner grocery or the post office with its flag. Should you happen upon one whose character has been obscured by insensitive "remuddling" or modernization, pause for a moment and look at its noble bones. The welcoming feeling of the structure defies attempts at alteration. As you look at it, try to imagine a time when its shelter provided a warm, embracing ambiance. Weatherwise—cool when hot and warm when cold—bungalows were and are a cozy retreat from the workaday world that still beckons to us all. The bungalow was, and is, an earthly manifestation of "heaven."

When whippoorwills call and ev'ning is nigh
I hurry to my blue heaven.
A turn to the right, a little white light
will lead you to my blue heaven.
You'll see a smiling face, a fireplace, a cozy room,
a little nest that's nestled where the roses bloom.
Just Mollie and me and baby makes three
We're happy in my blue heaven.

# The Craftsman Style
## VARIATIONS ON THE CLASSIC BUNGALOW

Reflecting its association with the Arts and Crafts Movement, the concept of Craftsman style came into general use when Gustav Stickley made it the title of his magazine, *The Craftsman,* which he published between 1901 and 1916. During those years, it came to be used as a kind of catch-all label, with applications to every aspect of a house and its interior. Its sources are found in traditional Japanese wood construction and the American Shingle and Stick styles of the nineteenth century. It is also the style most used for bungalow interiors.

Although *Arts and Crafts* is the term that is generally preferred, *Craftsman style* is also commonly used to refer to many related decorative arts of the period. It is significant that Stickley frequently applied the word "Craftsman" to many topics that appeared in his magazine. He promoted its progressive and practical innovations as a design philosophy, and even made an effort to extend them into the realm of social consciousness as a "Craftsman way of life." Gradually, however, the word took on its own momentum, going beyond any specific connections to Stickley's magazine or his work, and it came to be freely used by others as being characteristic of the period. "Craftsman" is still very much with us, and it is the style that is most associated with classic bungalows wherever they may be throughout the country.

Because of the bungalow's strong early links to the state, the terms *California Bungalow* or *California Craftsman* were sometimes applied to many houses that might otherwise be labeled simply "Craftsman." If it is not a direct ref-erence to the location of a house, the use of "California" in describing a bungalow has come to be most often linked with the later, simplified stucco examples of the 1920s, which proliferated there and elsewhere (fig. 77). There is no one single type of Craftsman home, but instead there are almost endless variations. The examples illustrated here will show the exceptional range and versatility of this style.

The most prominent element in the overall design of a bungalow is usually its roof, which defines the scale and presence of the house (fig. 32). Most often incorporating a variation of a gabled roof, the triangular gable ends of many bungalows feature substantial wood brackets, sometimes called knee-braces, which project under their eaves (figs. 30, 35, 55, 78). Sometimes massive beams are used without brackets, and some may appear overscaled for their apparent purpose (figs. 43, 45, 56, 59, 168). Despite the theory of honesty of construction and materials associated with the Arts and Crafts Movement, things are not always what they seem. Many architects and designers took considerable license in utilizing details that mimic actual structural elements, but are in fact only decorative (figs. 55, 58, 63). It may not always be apparent which elements are truly structural, but most were intended to appear that way. This same license was taken with some interior detailing and with Arts and Crafts furniture designs. Nevertheless, the Craftsman style almost always emphasizes structural elements as an integral part of its design. The style, sometimes rather austere, tends to minimize pure decoration in favor of elements that suggest

30. (*Opposite*) Detail of a bungalow porch in Healdsburg, California. From the street, the front porch is the feature that most defines the personality of a bungalow. In this example, sunlit flowers help define its perimeter. As an invitation to enter, its cool shadows offer shelter from the sun, and solace from the street. The broad, angular forms of the brackets and columns are familiar elements of the Craftsman design vocabulary. Seemingly skewered by the wooden porch railings, substantial clinker-brick piers support the columns and spreading roof.

strength and substance. Its major ornamentation is to be found in the beauty of the natural materials that have been used (figs. 53, 59, 60).

The prominence of one or more gables constitutes a typical format of Craftsman-style rooflines, and these may range from front-facing (fig. 30) to side-facing (fig. 32), cross-gabled (fig. 33) to double-front-gabled (figs. 35, 61), or some other variation of multigabled (figs. 34, 36, 42, 43, 47, 54, 55). The angle, or pitch, of these gabled roofs is often rather shallow, enhancing the feeling of horizontality that is associated with bungalow architecture. There is usually enough room for some kind of utilization of the attic level (figs. 31, 32, 44, 52, 65). Besides dormers, gable peaks are the other part of the building whose headroom dimensions determine how usable an attic space is, and they often contain an attic-level window (figs. 55, 59, 63, 69, 78, 79). Bungalow roofs spread themselves generously over the house, encompassing the form of the structure, and sheltering it like a broad awning or tent. The form of the front-porch roof is usually determined by that of the overall roof and may simply be an extension of that roof (figs. 30, 31, 32, 52, 56, 63, 65, 76). It could also be a restatement of the overall roof form on a smaller scale (figs. 33, 34, 35, 42, 46, 54). Sometimes the porch is actually fully recessed within the house walls, creating a loggia effect, when enclosed on three sides by full-height walls. A more typical recessed location is at a corner of the building, where only two of the house's walls define it (fig. 31).

The porch columns can be among the boldest elements of a bungalow's façade, and are subject to some extreme variations in style (figs. 53, 71). While their shapes and material finishes vary widely, the most common form is the square, tapering (or trapezoidal) column, usually of painted or stained wood, seen in many different proportions (figs. 30, 32, 33, 46, 47). This particular shape suggests strength by its weighty form, and its sloping silhouette implies the stability of a low center of gravity. A similar feeling is suggested by the use of battered, or sloping, exterior walls, a device that also serves to anchor the house visually to the ground. Such walls usually flare out fairly close to the ground, and suggest a feeling that the house is growing out of its site (figs. 80, 94, 141).

The common bungalow feature of deeply overhanging eaves provides shade to outside walls during the summer, and adds to the bungalow's distinctive profile and interplay of shadow lines (figs. 30, 35, 54, 55, 56). Deep eaves also provide a showcase for the rhythmic feature of exposed rafter ends or "rafter tails," which are frequently cut into curved or pointed profiles, so as to exaggerate them even more (figs. 32, 78, 80). The range of building materials in most Craftsman-style bungalows is predominated by the use of wood and its joinery. Wood shingling, with many possible variations of scale and texture, is a popular choice for exterior walls, as well as for a roofing material (figs. 36, 44, 58, 60).

The Craftsman style also incorporates the textural effects and colors inherent in river rock, which are random-sized stones that are usually gathered from a nearby creek or riverbed, and have been worn into smooth and rounded shapes (figs. 60, 64). Sometimes called cobblestones, river rock is often called arroyo stone in the West, a reference to the canyon-like riverbeds there, such as the Arroyo Seco in Pasadena. This stone was most often used in porch columns, house foundations, chimneys, and fireplace facings, and it forms a handsome contrast to the linearity and texture of woodwork (figs. 37, 54, 62, 63, 118, 174). Larger rocks with a rougher texture, usually referred to as boulders, were sometimes used in combination with smaller stones (figs. 58, 68, 103). Rocks and boulders were also important to bungalow landscaping, whether to complement existing stonework on the building, or to introduce a new material into the planting scheme (figs. 31, 33, 36, 86, 121, 154).

For a striking contrast, stones of varying sizes were sometimes combined with the craggy texture and deep color of clinker brick (fig. 61). This is the kind of brick most seen in Craftsman-style architecture, and it had even more design flexibility than river rock (figs. 1, 30, 70, 76, 155). Brick was also more readily available, should one be far from the arroyo or other sources that provided river rock. Although there are exceptions, of course, the use of solid brick for building houses was used more in the East and Midwest than in the West. "Face brick," a veneer of brick applied over a wood frame, is what is typically seen in brick bungalows (fig. 112). Besides the clinker variety, other brick colors, textures, and styles appeared both outside and inside a bungalow (figs. 7, 32, 33, 35, 36, 71, 72, 158). Brick was very popular for fireplace designs, especially the mixing together of multicolored bricks for an effect called "Tapestry Brick." Many brick mantel designs make use of the various textures possible from one color of brick, and use smooth bricks combined with those having a rough texture (fig. 175).

Lighting styles are more consistent. A simple and popular design of the period was a bowl made of glass (or sometimes metal) that was suspended by three or four chains (fig. 152). Sometimes the bowl was made of colored or molded glass to add interest to its surface. Other large, hanging fixtures were made of metal that was sometimes pierced and combined with colored glass, or sometimes had a fringed fabric shade and was hung low over the dining-room table (figs. 10, 138, 146, 160). Some interiors supplemented their table lamps by having electric-light sockets placed at the intersections of the ceiling beams, into which were screwed the clear filament-type bulbs that were common in early electrified interiors (figs. 138). These bare light bulbs were not criticized as they might be today; instead, they were admired for their "jewel-like" quality. These bare bulbs were sometimes enhanced by small glass or beaded shades that were placed close against the box beams. Also popular were small glass-shaded hanging lamps suspended on separate chains (figs. 39, 40, 49, 51, 135, 155, 159, 176). Such fixtures could also be mounted as wall sconces (figs. 66, 91, 133, 151, 169, 182) or arranged in other groupings as needed (figs. 67, 89, 187, 192). Fixtures with similar small shades were manufactured with large backplates flush-mounted against the ceiling, which anchored the hanging chains (fig. 38). Hand-wrought metal effects, usually in brass or copper that was patinated or antiqued, were the most desirable and characteristic metal finishes (figs. 72, 73, 74, 142, 170). Outdoor lights were usually variations on the hanging or wall- mounted lantern style, often with a squarish or trapezoidal shade, perhaps with decorative cutouts in the metal framework, or fitted with colored glass (figs. 43, 56, 59, 68, 132, 147, 178, 183, 191). With small overhanging "roof" forms, evoking miniature houses, some of the outdoor lanterns look strongly influenced by Japanese design, a harmonious complement to the Craftsman style (figs. 45, 124).

31. Bungalow in St. Helena, California. Dwarfed by a monumental redwood tree, the house extends a path of flower-bordered stepping stones in welcome. In the deepening dusk, the windows of the house glow like a lantern for the passerby. The turn-of-the-century design of this bungalow has been attributed to Bernard Maybeck (1862–1957). The garden was created by house resident and local landscaper John Abbott, who created the edgings of river rock to define the planting beds.

32. Bungalow in Sacramento, California. With a fringe of shaped rafter tails overhanging its porch and dormer, this 1911 house looks as if it had stepped out of the pages of a bungalow-plan book. Creating a variety of textures, both clinker and buff-colored brick complement the shingled and clapboard siding. An English carpenter named Jennings constructed the house and left behind a detailed journal of every building expense as a documentary record for the subsequent owners. A large oak tree has grown from the sapling that Mr. Jennings and his English bride planted when their son was born. The son still lives up the street, and he has provided the current owners with much house history and family lore.

33. The Austin bungalow, San Diego, California. In 1923, a local carpenter and cabinetmaker named Edgar B. Austin constructed this modest bungalow for himself. Acquired by the current owners in 1979 from the estate of Austin's wife, the house yielded an extraordinary treasure trove of carefully documented plans, permits, contracts, and invoices relating to its construction. In addition, its interiors are something of a time capsule. They boast the original Douglas fir woodwork, stained a gray-green—the color of weathered bark. The Wilton carpeting that first covered its floors remains in place today. Still heated by the original wood-burning parlor stove, it is unusual that the house has no fireplace. First subdivided in the 1860s, the neighborhood has been designated the Sherman Heights Historic District, and it includes a mixture of house styles.

34. Bungalow in Modesto, California. Wide shingled arches form a small gabled pavilion for the entry porch of this corner house. Two other bracketed gables intersect each other, and the higher one displays a flower box at its windows. Low walls form the railing of the porch, and as they divide at the entry steps, they combine with the arch to create a distinctive keyhole shape that frames the front door.

35. Bungalow in Oakland, California. The tautness of two front-facing gables lends crisp tension to the lines of this house. Complemented by the original windows, buff-colored brick, and a new landscaping scheme, the narrow clapboard siding contributes a delicate horizontal texture. Probably dating from about 1920, the overall form and straightforward detailing of this house is reminiscent of many plan-book examples.

36. The Keyes bungalow, Altadena, California. Nestled in the heart of a mountain community just above Pasadena, this classic example of an "airplane bungalow" hovers in its plot. Shingled walls and restrained detailing harmonize with the lush surroundings. A trio of dark upswept gable peaks forms a handsome contrast to the light-colored brick used in the foundation and in the piers and railings of the deep wraparound porch. Current owners Rod Holcomb and Jane Brackman have carried out an extensive and ongoing renovation of the 1911 house, with skilled carpenter/ builder James Holmes (now of Santa Fe) responsible for much of its implementation. This restoration work was started by the former owners, Mr. and Mrs. Ken Miedema, who were responsible for getting the house placed on the National Register of Historic Places.

37. Living room of the Keyes bungalow. This commodious room is entered from the porch through the wide glass-paned front door to the left. The first impression is one of a warmly generous space, lantern-hung beams, and a significant collection of American Arts and Crafts-period furniture and objects dispersed with a casual grace. Scattered rugs and cushions in vibrant American Indian patterns enliven honey-colored wood flooring and furniture. Framed into a series of tailored wall panels, a glowing butterscotch hue combines handsomely with adjacent natural oak and leather. The continuous deep umber band of the frieze area highlights the paler color of the ceiling panels.

38. Dining room of the Keyes bungalow. A pleasant tension between horizontal and vertical lines characterizes this room. The rich living-room color is restated in the dark horizontal panels just above the plate rail, a good foil for the dark patinated copper, pottery, and small landscape paintings on display there. Oak, with all its variations of color and grain, gives a rich warmth to the woodwork and furniture. The glass-fronted cabinets of the sideboard are filled with a set of reissued Roycroft china, and pieces of Arts and Crafts pottery are displayed below. Made of pierced metal shades over glass cylinders, the lights suspended over the table are given additional prominence by the substantial oak backplate.

39. Hallway of the Keyes bungalow. This meandering space reflects a planning concept used in the house, and its unusual form was created as a result. A row of bedrooms (to the right of this view) were placed so that each one extends several feet further into the hall space than the one that precedes it. By placing front-facing windows near the successive outside corners created by this arrangement, each bedroom gains a view toward the front garden. Serving as the spine of the house, and fostering good air circulation, this hallway connects the living room to every other room, as well as to an enclosed stairway leading to the attic level. The color scheme established in the living and dining rooms extends into the hallway, which also has some built-ins.

40. Kitchen of the Keyes bungalow. Carefully following period design, this kitchen renovation employs materials and planning of the time that had been obscured by subsequent modernization. The result is characterized by utility, understatement, and authenticity of detail. Both ceramic tile and wood are combined on the walls. Commodious floor-to-ceiling cabinets and a hardwood floor complete the effect. The lighting, hardware, and appliances are historically appropriate. Useful for kitchen tasks, the large central table also accommodates informal family dining. The dining room is at the left of this view, with the hallway reached from the center door, and the door at the right leads to the utility porch.

41. Bathroom of the Keyes bungalow. Original period fixtures continue to perform efficiently here. A pair of small casement windows, flanking a mirrored medicine cabinet above the pedestal sink, provide light and air where most needed. Additional mechanical ventilation has been concealed behind the wood backplate of the ceiling light.

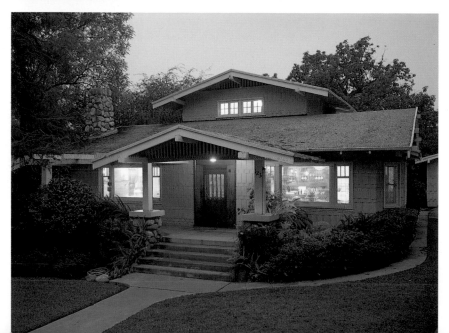

42. Twycross house, Sierra Madre, California. Casting a welcoming glow in the advancing twilight, the raised attic-level room shows that this is an "airplane bungalow." Constructed on three lots in 1914 by Converse and Ruth Twycross, the house stayed in the same family until 1987. Although the property's zoning allowed for higher-density development, a particularly appropriate adaptive reuse was realized when the house became office space for *American Bungalow* magazine.

43. Bungalow in San Diego, California. Built in the North Park section of town, this corner house was constructed in 1919. The present pale color scheme shows off its basic forms well, but it is likely that the house once boasted deeper shadows. An almost Prairie-style influence is suggested in thick, squared porch columns that extend directly to the ground. Although the detailing of the house is in the Craftsman style, it achieves an almost abstract severity.

44. Bungalow in Berkeley, California. Freshened by new shingles, this little house shines like a new-minted penny in the surrounding greenery. Here is a charming, minimal version of the Craftsman style.

45. Detail of a front porch, Pasadena, California. The cantilevered roof overhang that shelters this entry merely implies a porch, distilled to its essence. Built in 1905 by the design and contracting firm of Grable and Austin, the house shows evidence of a sophisticated designer's hand in the use of rows of oversized shingles aligned with a band of casement windows of similar size. Their exaggerated scale shows one of the dramatic ways that shingles can be used in architectural applications that go beyond surface decoration. In contrast to the deep blue-green of the shingles, a warmer wood stain is used on the door casing, window sash, porch overhang, and latticed gable vent. Large square pegs are found on both the copper hinges and wooden planks of the front door, a handsome reference to the Craftsman aesthetic of emphasizing structural forms in lieu of ornament.

46. Bungalow in Pasadena, California. Located in the Bungalow Heaven Landmark District, this house catches the last rays of the afternoon sun. Seeming to emphasize a wide and spreading quality, the roof line is distinguished by the two different gable angles. The feeling of horizontality is even more pronounced because of its low foundation, and the massive tapering columns seem formidable enough to support the entire house.

47. Bungalow in Pasadena, California. In late 1914, a building permit was filed for this home to be built in what is now the Bungalow Heaven Landmark District. The original owners, the Reverend and Mrs. Cornelius N. Wester, probably selected the design from a plan book. Full-height, tapering stucco columns define its wraparound porch. Each column is embellished on its outer face with a brick inset of linear design. Both the living and dining rooms have direct access to the porch. Flattened, intersecting gables create roof interest. Reverend Wester died in 1937, but his wife remained here through 1955. The house has since undergone a meticulous restoration, inside and out, by current owners Ken Miedema and Julie Reiz.

48. The Kenfield house, Berkeley, California. City records show that this house may have been built as early as 1905, and it is first associated with Stephen Kenfield, a local builder and developer, who owned this and a considerable amount of adjacent property. Its architect has never been conclusively identified, but neighborhood lore has established that architect Bernard Maybeck, who lived four blocks away, was seen at its construction site. It is known to have been occupied by a Theodore Sherwood and his family by 1908, and the Sherwoods apparently kept several farm animals on the premises. Behind a rustic fence and garden gate, the house peeks from behind a veil of greenery, and is almost hidden from the street. Its compact design uses board-and-batten siding and shingles, and features a corner bay inset with green stained glass, which forms a cozy bedroom window seat (fig. 51).

49. Kenfield house living room (with the dining room at the left). Distinguished by its handsome and original all-redwood interior, each of the main living areas has a peaked and beamed ceiling. At the far end of the living room, a small entry hall is visible, with the front door and porch to the right. The broad opening between the living and dining rooms, a typical feature of bungalows, may be closed by french doors that fold back on either side. The finely detailed redwood surfaces form an ideal backdrop for the extensive collection of Arts and Crafts pottery, furniture, textiles, and California landscape paintings. The lighting fixtures are also of the period.

50. Detail of the Kenfield house living room. The appealing combination of both rusticity and richness that redwood brings to this interior is evident here. The small side chair, an unusual design by the Stickley Brothers (of Grand Rapids, Michigan) shows an English Arts and Crafts influence, and the small bookcase is a Gustav Stickley design. One of the vintage books it contains is a Nancy Drew adventure called *The Bungalow Mystery* by Carolyn Keene. On top of the bookcase is a Weller Coppertone vase with a whimsical frog motif.

51. Kenfield house bedroom. Another masterful wood-working effort, this room's ceiling appears to be an abstract version of an English hammerbeam roof. The hanging light fixtures are of the period. The armoire is by Liberty of London, and it is decorated with Ruskin Pottery ceramic insets set in a line across its top. The design of the chair standing next to the armoire was created for the 1894 Swedenborgian Church in San Francisco, an early Arts and Crafts landmark. The chair, attributed to Bernard Maybeck, is often considered to be the forerunner of all so-called "Mission" furniture. Similar versions were reproduced after 1894 by Joseph P. McHugh and Company and others. The chair by the bed is an English Arts and Crafts design in a more delicate scale.

52. Bungalow in St. Helena, California. The outdoor living room, or porch, of this house is framed by morning-glory vines, which hide unusual porch columns of unpeeled redwood logs. The house is owned by long-time San Bruno mayor Bob Marshall and wife Paula, who restored it with the help of Darrell Galusha. The Marshalls bought the house from a local family of merchants named Goodman, who had owned it for many years, and attribute its design to Bernard Maybeck. It dates from around the turn of the century.

53. Detail of log porch column, St. Helena, California. This cluster of unpeeled redwood logs forming one of the porch columns of this turn-of-the-century house is typical of the Adirondack style popular in vacation architecture.

54. Bungalow porches in Alameda, California. At the left is a classic example of Craftsman style, with its trapezoidal river-rock porch piers and structural timber dramatically displayed. Its cropped or jerkin-headed gables show English influence, and the porch railing seems deliberately underscaled to make the adjacent elements appear more forceful. Both houses were built around 1920, and the small house at the right is derived from the Prairie style.

55. Bungalow in Alameda, California. The prow-like eaves of the multiple gables of this house are canted forward in a dynamic gesture. Below them, a profusion of oversized brace-like brackets, crossbars and zigzag wood banding shows traces of the Stick and Eastlake architectural styles. The height of the porch openings aligning with that of the living-room windows emphasizes horizontality. Wide clapboard siding continues that emphasis in a sturdy-looking base for the design. With its deep eaves spanned by a small pergola structure, the large front-facing gable opens onto a small hidden deck.

56. Bungalow in Pasadena, California. Located in the Bungalow Heaven Landmark District, the impressive overhanging front-porch timber work of this house is held aloft by massive brick and stucco piers. Direct access is possible from the porch to the dining room (adjacent to the Adirondack chair) and to the living room at the right. Designed and built in 1913 for two sisters, Margaret and Isabel Hamilton, it is the work of the local firm of Keift and Hethrington. With widely spreading lines, the textural interest of its shingled exterior walls in a dark stain is enlivened by the deep blue-green used for the door and window trim.

57. Living room of the bungalow in figure 56. Stepping inside this house, the comforts of its living room are immediately apparent. Typical bungalow features include a pair of small windows at the far end above built-in bookcases, flanking the focal point of a Batchelder tile-faced fireplace. A collection of appropriate Arts and Crafts furniture and objects are well integrated into the room. To the right is a so-called Chicago Window, characterized by a large central pane and two smaller windows on either side that can open. This type of window was popular for providing a flexibility of ventilation and a maximum of light. Its broad form is seen in the work of progressive Chicago School architects such as Louis Sullivan, who used it as a window module in some of their early skyscraper office-building projects.

58. Bungalow in Monrovia, California. A whimsical use of boulders that delineate the property emphasizes the appeal of this Craftsman-style classic. The extensive use of stone in its foundation, lower walls, and chimney was made possible by the convenient local source of this material, for rock-strewn arroyos descend from the mountains behind. A broad, flattened dormer peeks out over an extended pergola structure. The living room, located at the left, features a beamed ceiling that is open to the peak of its roof ridge. Original lighting, on swagged chains, is dramatically hung down the middle of the room.

59. (*Opposite*) Front porch of a bungalow in Benicia, California. Massive timbers, incorporated into the compact pergola-style entry porch, are set on a low river-rock foundation. The wooden cover on this low wall can be used for the display of potted plants, or can double as a bench for casual seating. With a hint of warmth and comfort within, the sun's last rays set the textures of the house aglow. Also see figure 60.

60. Bungalow in Benicia, California. With its symphony of textures beautifully distilled in the Craftsman style, this unique house invites a closer look. It took a year to construct the house to the design of an Oakland architect named Smith, and it was completed in 1911. The original owner, a local dentist named Dr. White, was persuaded to sell it soon after its construction to the Barkley family, and it remained in their hands until the mid-1970s, when it was purchased by the current owner. With an unusually high river-rock foundation that rises above the height of the main floor level the rounded forms of the rock are emphasized by the serpentine boxwood hedge. Pronounced horizontal emphasis is reinforced by double courses of shingles, in alternating widths, which contribute a warmly varied texture. In the shadows of deep eaves in the gables board-and-batten siding adds strongly to the textural interest of the house that also has a tall chimney made of clinker brick.

61. Bungalow in Pasadena, California. This striking house, constructed in 1912 by a local contractor named Walter A. Waldock, is located in the Bungalow Heaven Landmark District. Waldock reportedly spent $2,200 on it, and was responsible for building ten other homes in the neighborhood. The Arroyo Seco boulders and clinker brick are combined in a deliberately picturesque way, sometimes described as the "peanut-brittle" style. Complemented by two matching porch piers, the massive chimney rises to extend through the projecting eaves. The façade is handsomely double-gabled, but most of the house is contained within the sweep of the main gable. The building systems and the foundation were rebuilt in an extensive restoration by the previous architect-owner, Tony Kwok. All stonework, including an inglenook fireplace, was painstakingly dismantled, numbered, and reassembled after extensive seismic reinforcement.

62. Detail of a bungalow porch, Sacramento, California. This is actually the side façade of the house, and it features a deep wraparound porch and a procession of massive river-rock columns that merge with the foundation. The serpentine planting bed separates the house from the lawn. From the middle of the columns oversized braces support the overhang of the roof. A small open deck, which is set into the roof above the porch, is enclosed by a low shingled wall.

63. Bungalow in San Jose, California. The design of this house is close to that illustrated in figure 1, as well as being remarkably similar to the plan-book design (fig. 2) by Henry L. Wilson. Lacking the upswept gable peak and clinker brick of those two houses, it does share the similarities of its overall form, as well as mortise-and-tenon details on the paired columns, and swagged chains between the porch piers. This kind of chain-railing treatment is most often found between brick or stone piers, but doesn't always survive. The Naglee Park neighborhood of San Jose is blessed with many significant houses of the Arts and Crafts period.

64. Bungalow in Highland Park (part of Los Angeles),California. This extraordinary stone-covered house is located on a street that was known as Professor's Row, named for the shared occupation of a number of its residents at the turn of the century. The street is close to the former site of Occidental College, and was at that time part of a colony of artists and craftspeople. The house, officially declared a Los Angeles landmark in 1988, was built in the 1890s by Elizabeth Young Gordon, wife of the vice president of the college. She was also responsible for developing other homes in the neighborhood. The stonework of this house demonstrates how early the Arts and Crafts influence was already seen in local home design. Incorporated into an overall architectural plan that has some late Victorian vestiges of proportion and detail, its window sash is similar to designs seen on some late Queen Anne and Colonial Revival houses. Nevertheless, with its stonework, exposed rafter tails, and front porch, the bungalow is infused with an Arts and Crafts sensibility. Paved with Batchelder-tile seconds obtained from that company's nearby factory, an open patio area added later in front of the porch is an interesting complement to the house.

65. Bungalow in Oakland, California. The orderly grid of small panes in the glass wind-screen to the left of the front door is duplicated in the casement windows elsewhere on the façade. The side-facing gabled roof, interrupted by a large protruding dormer, is a typical Craftsman bungalow form. A muted paint scheme allows the building to blend in with its leafy surroundings.

66. Entry hall seen from the living room of the Oakland bungalow. With a built-in bench and a tiny oriel window, the entry hall is divided from the adjacent living room by partially slatted screen walls. Slats also are used at the left side of the bench, which has a seat that lifts up for storage space. The frieze is a wallpaper adaptation of the Roycroft china pattern attributed to Dard Hunter. The high wooden wainscot and plate rail continues into the dining room at the right. The oak floors are bordered with bands of dark wood in all of the main living areas.

61

67. Living room of the Oakland bungalow. In this view toward the front of the house, one looks through the living room to the small library/study, with its built-in bookcases. This room has a high wainscot and wallpaper frieze that matches that of the entry hall, which is just out of view to the right. Simple Roman shades of tailored canvas closely match the pale cream-colored walls, providing dramatic contrast to the dark wood trim and box beams. The entry to the dining room, from which this view was taken, may be closed off by sliding pocket doors.

68. The Batchelder house, Pasadena, California. The softly variegated hues of the tiled walkway, with an occasional figural inset, are clues to the identity of this house. A small tile panel, set into the stucco of the stone-encrusted chimney, offers another clue. Overlooking the Arroyo Seco, the house was designed and built in 1909 by Ernest A. Batchelder (1875–1957), the celebrated manufacturer of Arts and Crafts tiles. He lived here with his wife until financial reversals in the Depression era and her death prompted him to rent it out. He then moved into separate guest quarters that adjoined a garage (fig. 24), which had been built on the property in the late Twenties. The original kiln structure, where he began his tile business, still stands on the premises. The façade of the house is defined by a projecting single-story living room, whose interior boasts an open-peaked roof and a tall fireplace with a superbly tiled facing. Not a true bungalow, the bedroom story of the house is visible beyond, with a wide sleeping porch stretched across its upper gable. In addition to his fame in the tile business, Batchelder was also a noted design educator, and influenced many creative minds of the period through his teachings and writings. Before his tile career took off, he was Director of Art at the progressive Throop Polytechnic Institute in Pasadena.

69. Bungalow in Moss Beach, California. Weathered by time and tide, this shingled home has braved the elements from its cliffside perch since about 1908. Its massive river-rock chimney is trimmed in red brick and is further embellished with a decorative inset and boulder crown. The front porch, glassed in to deflect the continual winds off the Pacific, provides a perfect place to admire panoramic sunsets and cloudscapes over the ocean.

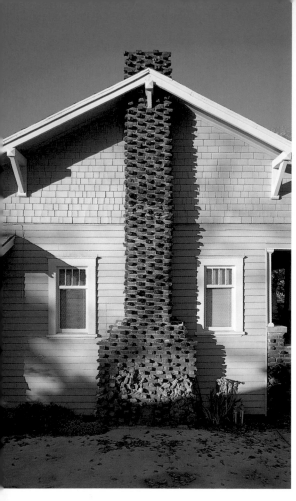

70. Detail of a bungalow in Modesto, California. The extraordinary textural effects that can be achieved with clinker brick made it a popular component of Arts and Crafts architecture. This chimney shows a dramatic bricklaying pattern that utilizes alternating ends and sides of individual bricks to create its surface interest. The projecting brick ends, rough and misshapen, are shown off in high relief as they project from the face of the adjacent bricks. At the base of the chimney are several irregular chunks of fused brick, which have been incorporated into the overall design, and almost appear to have grown out of the ground. The term *clinker brick* was coined from a clinking sound made during brick manufacturing, which occurred when some bricks, placed too close to the heat source in the oven, began to crack and vitrify (or melt). Originally sold as seconds or discarded by brick factories, the surprisingly decorative properties of clinkers became evident, and they also came to be used in combination with stone and other types of brick.

71. Detail of a bungalow in San Diego, California. Sure to be a standout on any corner, this 1911 house is situated on one in the North Park area, which shows off its exceptional brick porch piers to great advantage. Seeming to emerge from the ground as monumental trapezoids of two-toned brick, these rise and reshape themselves into square vertical piers that support the porch roof. The porch railing contains a planter for floral display. The oversized trusses and projecting beams of the roof of the porch seem to float above the giant piers on short, almost inconsequential, wooden posts.

72. Detail of a bungalow in Alhambra, California. Sturdily proportioned, the engaged square brick column of this rather austere porch mirrors a free-standing one just out of view at the outside corner of the porch. An original copper ceiling fixture casts a glow on the natural wood tongue-and-groove ceiling, and is a prelude to more original lighting fixtures inside. The house and its neighboring twin were built in 1910 by two sisters. In 1987, it was sold to the present owners by the original family.

73. Detail of the living room in the Alhambra bungalow. Across the front window hang embroidered and appliquéd linen curtains, recently recreated by Dianne Ayres, which are decorated with a tree motif in Arts and Crafts style. One of a pair in the room, the individual lights of the exceptional hanging copper fixture match those seen on the front porch. The shallow copper bowls are suspended from chains, and can be raised or lowered. The hand-hammered finish emphasizes their craft appeal. Although the maker is not known, the fixtures are believed to be the work of a skilled local metalsmith.

74. Detail of the dining room in the Alhambra bungalow. The artisan that created the copper living-room fixtures (fig. 73) probably made the copper lamps that rise from each end of a built-in sideboard. Four vertical copper supports are atttached to the corners of the square mounting post, and they support an openwork shade of hand-hammered copper grapes and leaves, which are also repeated in a chandelier over the center table. The panels of the wainscot have been inset with a Bradbury & Bradbury adaptation of a William Morris wallpaper pattern of stylized willow branches.

75. Detail of the living room in the Alhambra bungalow. Above a fireplace of simple lines and rather plain brick facing, a fine inset panel of repoussé copper work depicts a tranquil landscape. This treasure was quite possibly made by the same unknown artisan responsible for the extraordinary lighting fixtures.

76. Bungalow in Albany, California. Backlit by the moon, this handsomely detailed 1917 house gains visual importance from its lofty siting, and its rustic stone staircase almost appears to be carved from the rocky hillside. Believed to have worked with Bernard Maybeck, to whom the design of the house is attributed, its original owner was a local building contractor named Madrid. As the first house to be built in this neighborhood, its promontory offered a sweeping view that is now best seen from its attic dormer. The shingles over the porch have been set at angles to reflect the form of its opening, and adjacent clinker brick is a familiar detail. A suggestion of Oriental influence is seen in the fretwork-style porch railing and in the roof's gentle upward sweep.

77. Bungalow in Petaluma, California. In response to its corner site, a bold entry stair spills forth from this California Bungalow. The term *California Bungalow*, which is usually associated with stucco walls and simplified Craftsman detailing, is sometimes used as a general term to describe similar bungalows, wherever they may be located. The house dates to 1926, the decade in which the bungalow peaked in popularity. This hillside location created the bonus of a usable "daylight" basement, and it was well utilized by its first occupants, a couple who made a living fabricating pots and pans there for the next sixty years. There is a slight hint of a Mediterranean influence in the combination of stucco and modified arches on the porch, and in the ornamental brick-trimmed parapet over the stairway.

78. Bungalow in Sacramento, California. Built in 1920, this cross-gabled house has a ground level of sufficient height to have been developed into additional living space. Springing from a narrow clapboard-covered lower level and tall piers, the square tapered columns are repeated as pilasters flanking the front door and windows.

79. Bungalow in Benicia, California. This vibrantly colored bungalow sits up higher than most, with its "daylight" basement window peering through a tangle of greenery that links it to the ground. The front door's oval glass panel, flanked by sidelights, is a reference to the Colonial Revival style, which also favored this kind of narrow clapboard siding. An Italian-style garden in back inspired the paint colors.

80. Bungalow in San Jose, California. In 1907, a doctor named Capp, who specialized in homeopathic medicine, chose to construct a home and office in the respectable Naglee Park district. A corner location and picket fence emphasizes the rambling lines of this roomy house, which is actually a courtyard or patio house. This architectural arrangement divides the interior into both public and private spaces. Patio bungalows were best suited to mild climates, as they tended to be more difficult to heat. But they promoted good air circulation, ideal in hot weather, and so were favored in early California hacienda architecture for that reason. The slightly battered, or flared, base at the house's foundation echoes the decorative window casings and hipped roof. The handsome porch has a pair of built-in benches.

# Other Influences on Bungalow Style

While the majority of bungalow designs are in the Craftsman style, there are a number of other stylistic influences to be seen. Usually such variations reflect a desire to achieve variety, novelty, or possibly to comply with a request of the client (fig. 21). Variations were much used in developments where bungalows were built for speculation, and their exterior personality, or curb appeal, helped to sell them. Ever-changing fashion and public taste were important factors in tracing the evolution of the bungalow's outward appearance. While many style variations appear in combination with features that are predominantly Craftsman, some influences entirely redefine the style of the house. This is particularly found in some Mission Revival, Spanish Colonial Revival, or Prairie houses. While these variations are a potential source of confusion, it is useful to remember that bungalows are technically defined by interior-planning characteristics, rather than outward appearance. There are more bungalows out there than meet the eye. The following examples only hint at their sheer variety.

### SWISS CHALET STYLE
#### (Figures 81–91)

Although the Swiss Chalet style appears to be just a variant of the Craftsman style, it is a definite and important influence to recognize. Characteristic of the Swiss Chalet style is a large, single forward-facing gable that allows the roof to hover low over the building. The façade of such a house is usually further defined by particularly deep overhanging eaves, and structural roof elements (possibly decorated). In general, there is a more ornamental quality to the detailing of Swiss-derived houses. The use of wood is emphasized over all other materials. Rather than relying on structural elements alone to express the design, detailing may include the use of decoratively carved linear moldings (fig. 83), beam ends, rafter tails, or bargeboards. One of the easiest Swiss Chalet features to detect in what is basically a Craftsman design is the use of decorative cut-out designs in its porch or balcony railings. Such railings are made of plain upright boards (set closely or edge-to-edge), and sometimes they have shapes created by the combined effect of two adjacent cutouts (figs. 81, 86, 191). Other common Swiss Chalet details are the use of vertical siding in the upper gable (fig. 81), and flower boxes added to the façade (fig. 82).

### ENGLISH TUDOR, ENGLISH COTTAGE, AND COLONIAL REVIVAL STYLES
#### (Figures 92–98)

English style was a major influence on bungalow design. Most easily recognized is probably the use of half-timbering (fig. 93), which in the Twenties was more often used on large-scale houses than on modest bungalows. This gave rise to the soubriquet of Stockbroker Tudor, which not only described the style of such houses, but also acknowledged the source of funds for some who built them. The most prominent English influence on bungalows was some variant of the "cottage style," with its traditional feeling of "hearth-and-hominess." The early-twentieth century saw an increasing consumer interest in such evocations of quaintness. Rounded roof lines were based on the forms of thatched roofs (figs. 15, 92, 96), sometimes with shingles specially built up and contoured. Often this was combined with clipped or cut-off gable ends, called "jerkin-headed" gables (figs. 95, 96). This roof form was sometimes used as a device to reduce the apparent size of the roof. Trellises (fig. 95) appear on many bungalows that are inspired by the English cottage. Diamond-paned windows (fig. 94), used on some Colonial Revival houses, are another English influence. Although not as commonly used on very modest houses, in many parts of the country the use of red brick and white trim is a standard way of suggesting the Colonial Georgian or Palladian styles of the eighteenth century. Colonial Revival bungalows (fig. 97) are often styled with columns, narrow clapboard siding, and classical moldings. When used just as accent elements, the columns may sometimes be the only element of a design that refer to the Colonial Revival style (figs. 28, 98).

## MISSION REVIVAL AND SPANISH COLONIAL REVIVAL STYLES `(Figures 99–112)

These related styles may share some features (such as the characteristic arch, textured-stucco wall finishes, and variations of the red-tile roof), but there are certain differences that help identify each influence. The Mission Revival style was the first to develop, and was inspired by the designs of the eighteenth-century missions built in early California and the Southwest. These buildings were typically of adobe construction and were fairly primitive in their detailing and finishes. Although rough, the buildings had traces of the more sophisticated Spanish Baroque forms that had earlier

81. Bungalow in Berkeley, California. Evident in the verticality and pointed ends of the wood siding in the front gable, and in the flat cutout forms used on the railings at the porch and upstairs windows, the influence of the Swiss Chalet style (sometimes called only "Chalet") pervades this cheerful house. The current owners, here for over twenty years, have found that it was built in 1910 for $1,500 by Carl Eriksson, a local builder, who was active in the neighborhood between 1908 and 1912. Random-size fieldstones, more roughly textured than river rock, are used for the prominent front chimney and porch piers. Featuring a pair of built-in benches between the stone piers at the left, the recessed porch is expanded visually with a shallow pergola that extends across half the façade.

traveled to this hemisphere from Spain and Portugal. The Mission Revival style tends to emphasize the façade, often extending it upward to form an arched, S-curved or angled parapet against the sky (figs. 27, 99, 110), as did many historic missions. Sometimes the tops of house dormers have smaller versions of such parapets. Roof overhangs are generally deep, and arcaded porches are characteristic (fig. 100). The general feeling of the Mission Revival style is one of substance (fig. 108) and is more typical of the larger houses than of bungalows.

The Spanish Colonial Revival style emerged after the 1915 Panama-Pacific Exposition in San Diego, where it was used as that event's thematic style. The influential buildings at the Exposition were more refined (and historically accurate) interpretations of those Spanish Baroque buildings that had long existed throughout Latin America. The style soon became popular, especially in the West and South, and received indirect promotion by association with Hollywood and its emerging movie industry (fig. 101). Characterized by a freer use of ornamental forms, it could also combine with such other influences as Moorish, Gothic, Italian, or Mediterranean (fig. 103) for novelty effects. Courtyard or patio-style planning, rambling compositions of forms, and details like wrought-iron or turned-wood window grills, added to the element of fantasy. Porch elements are sometimes reduced to only a small shed roof over the front door, and eaves usually have very little overhang. Colorful glazed tiles were used on wall areas as accents, and also for decorative floors. Roof shapes varied from flat, to gable-ended, to hipped. Multiple combinations of these occurred even on small houses, and sometimes included tower forms to add to their picturesque outline (figs. 16, 19, 20, and 21).

## PRAIRIE STYLE
### (Figures 113–117)

Often associated with the Chicago School and the early work of Frank Lloyd Wright, this style emerged in the American Midwest at the beginning of this century, and included the work of many architects. Although the basic premise of relating a structure to its site is one shared by different stylistic approaches that contributed to the evolution of bungalow architecture, a new (and particularly American) style was born out of an attempt to relate a house design to the spreading horizon that dominates our Midwestern landscape. Porches and terraces sometimes are used to further this connection. The Midwestern versions of the Prairie style are usually made of brick, but stucco versions often appear elsewhere. Driven by a relentless quest to emphasize the horizontal line, Prairie-style roofs may appear almost flat, but most often they are hipped with a very shallow pitch (fig. 114). Characterized

by their sheltering overhangs, the eaves tend to conceal the clutter of any projecting rafter tails behind squared fascia boards, and are typically cantilevered (figs. 116, 117). Porches are often supported by massive, squared columns that are very simply detailed, with perhaps a square-edged overhang at the top (figs. 113, 117). Sometimes large, architectural-looking (and usually concrete) planters with shapes that repeat some element of the house, punctuate the porches or terraces. Helping to relieve the severity of some Prairie houses is the use of simply designed, predominantly geometric art-glass windows as accents (fig. 113).

## ORIENTAL STYLE
### (Figures 118–122)

This influence, found in some of the earliest examples of bungalow architecture, forms a comfortable, logical complement to the Craftsman style. Perhaps this is because the structural emphasis of the Craftsman style was partly influenced by Japanese timber construction. Traditionally perceived as somewhat exotic and mysterious, Asian design has interested Americans since the earliest days of the China Trade in the seventeenth century. After Japan's self-imposed period of isolation from the rest of the world of over two hundred years, the specific interest in that country grew rapidly after trade was finally re-established in the 1850s. At the various World Fair expositions that occurred in the late-nineteenth and early-twentieth centuries, many people were able to see a number of authentically built structures from distant lands. Buildings erected by the Japanese were especially admired and studied. The architects Greene and Greene and Frank Lloyd Wright were particularly impressed with Japanese structures, and their own work shows evidence of that interest. The Japanese influence is also seen in the work of many others, including anonymous designers of modest bungalows, whose plan-book schemes were used to build so many of them. The most common evidence of the Oriental influence is to be seen in the upswept gable peaks (figs. 119–122), reminiscent of those seen on pagodas. This feature may appear on what is otherwise a Craftsman house (figs. 1, 36). Although less specifically, the detailing of exposed timberwork on some Craftsman houses recalls robust Japanese wood construction (fig. 56). More outlandishly Oriental effects were also employed. Pagoda-derived forms were used in roof beams, rafter tails, columns, and in other detailing (figs. 120, 122). While Japan seems to be a primary source for most of the exotic influences seen in bungalow architecture, origins aren't always clear (fig. 118), so use of the more general description of Oriental style usually covers these variations.

82. Chalet-style house, Highland Park (part of Los Angeles), California. Featuring the lowered eaves and wide, front-gabled roofline that characterize many Chalet-style houses, this design is very simply detailed. Its knee-brace brackets are unpainted wood, which blend well with its natural shingled texture. Although larger than a true bungalow, its feeling is very similar. The original owner, Mary P. Field, had the house built in 1903 on Professor's Row, near the former site of Occidental College. Flower planters relieve the façade's austerity. The house became an official Los Angeles landmark in 1988.

83. Chalet-style house, Vallejo, California. Designed by famous Bay Area architect Julia Morgan (1872–1957), this spectacular house was constructed between 1907 and 1909. Showcased by its hilltop siting and large scale, Swiss Chalet features are seen in the wide, front-facing gable with its deep overhangs, decoratively shaped and cut-out brackets under the eaves, and bands of ornamentally embellished wood trim outlining the roof edges, attic level, and second-floor balcony. Other style influences are from the Colonial Revival, seen in the entry porch and window detailing, and the Craftsman-derived use of exposed structural elements, seen in the rafter tails and adjacent roof beams. Morgan's best-known work is William Randolph Hearst's castle at San Simeon, California.

84. Mariposa, formerly the Frost-Tufts house (1911), Hollywood, California. Designed by Arthur R. Kelly for Dr. C.L. Frost, and set in a secluded canyon site in the hills above Hollywood, a photograph of this house was published shortly after its completion. It was described as having been inspired by the Swiss chalet and illustrated in *Bungalows*, a popular design-advice book of the day by Henry H. Saylor, who was enthusiastic about the way the architect had sited the house successfully in steep terrain. Kelly worked for the offices of Greene and Greene, but he had produced this design on his own. Begun in 1905, the project was completed over a five-year period. The house had been occupied since Dr. Frost's death in 1966 by his daughter Kate Frost Tufts. It was recently sold to its current owner, Hollywood film producer Monty Montgomery.

85. Floor plans of Mariposa, formerly the Frost-Tufts house (1911). Having been published with the exterior photograph (fig. 84), the floor plans emphasize a design strongly influenced by the landscape. In the first-floor plan (at left), the curving hillside is addressed by the angled placement of the dining room (fig. 89), the kitchen (fig. 90), and service areas to one side of the central living room (fig. 88). Soon after the house was built, Dr. Frost had Arthur Kelly add a sun room off the dining room, which is shown here as part of the open front terrace. At the same time, a sleeping porch was added to the master bedroom on the second floor at the right. The front second-floor balcony has access from both the master bedroom and the nursery.

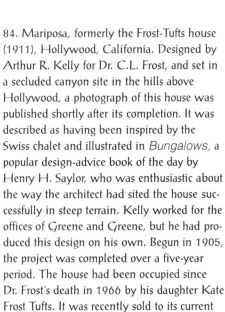

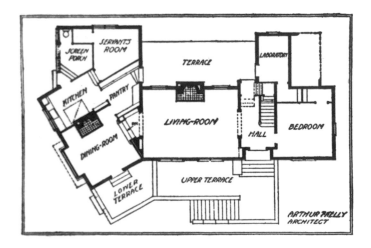

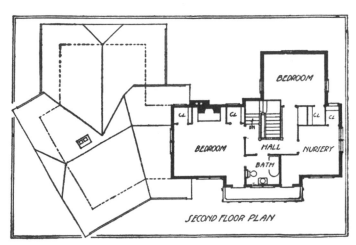

86. Mariposa, Hollywood, California. The original design integrity of the house and its grounds has been the subject of a meticulous restoration by its present owner. The fusion of the building to its hillside site is particularly apparent in this photograph. Natural rock has been fashioned into rustic flights of stairs that meander through the grounds and up to the house. Adding visual weight to its foundation, the enclosing shingled walls of the front deck and prominent entry stairs extend the structure further into the landscape. The Swiss Chalet influence, apparent in the cutout designs of the second-floor balcony railing, is also prominent in the wide, spreading roof of the central gable. Sheltered by this balcony's overhang, the front door is slightly recessed into the façade. In the angled end of the house at left, the enclosed sun porch adjoins the dining room (fig. 89). The project's restoration architect was Martin Eli Weil, and the extensive landscaping scheme was created by Sarah Munster.

87. Mariposa guest house. Just out of view of the main house, this small board-and-batten bungalow is nestled into a setting of drought-tolerant landscaping. Multiple sets of French doors lead to a large living room with a fireplace at its far end. The color of the board and batten, in combination with natural wood trim, chimney brick, and garden stonework, harmonizes with the muted desert colors of succulents and cacti in the surrounding landscape.

88. Mariposa living room. The interior of the house immediately establishes its warm character of welcoming informality and comfort. Under the tailored, linear design of the wood ceiling, the activity of the house centers around this room. The dining room, which has been set at an angle to the axis of the living room, is visible through the wide doorway. Carefully recreating its original appearance and application, a natural-color burlap wallcovering has been installed directly over the wide wooden planks that sheathe the walls. Built-in bookcases with open fronts invite browsing, and they flank the doorway openings at either end of the room. Next to the fireplace, the unusual combination of bird's-eye and tiger maple is seen in a Roycroft Morris chair, which was part of the original maple furnishings of the "Ralph Waldo Emerson" bedroom at the Roycroft Inn in East Aurora, New York. Visible just to the left of the chair, and once part of the Inn's dining-hall furnishings, is an Ali Baba bench (the name of its Roycroft craftsman). Behind the sofa is an octagonal leather-topped table by Gustav Stickley. Color and pattern is introduced by a lively array of Navajo rugs. Roger L. Conant Williams was the designer/curator/Arts and Crafts consultant on this project.

89. Mariposa dining room. With an oversized central panel oriented toward the view, the shallow bay window that forms this end of the house has unusually narrow side windows, which open for ventilation. French doors open to the sun porch at the left, a quiet retreat with wicker furniture that leads out to the front terrace. The chestnut dining table and oak leather-backed chairs at the window are by Onondaga Shops. The oak ladderback chairs are by Gustav Stickley, who also made the small oak trestle table at the window. The oak sideboard in the corner was produced during Gustav Stickley's experimental United Crafts period, just after the turn of the century.

90. Mariposa kitchen. A restrained statement in the style of the period, the kitchen has been little changed from its original appearance. The essentials of good natural light and ventilation are provided by a trio of casement windows above the sink. Supplemental lighting is provided by a pair of nickel-plated wall sconces and suspended Holophane glass work lights. The cabinets and hardware are faithful to period designs, and one to the left of the sink conceals a dishwasher. The cabinets at right frame a doorway leading to the back porch and to a servant's room (as named on the house plan). A cabinet-lined pantry divides the kitchen from the dining room.

91. Mariposa master bedroom. Tucked into the sloping roof-line, its leafy outlook shaded by overhanging eaves, the master bedroom has the character of a hideaway space. The French doors lead to a sleeping porch, which is now used as a light-filled study. There is a fireplace at the right opposite the windows, and adjoining the room is a bath with original fixtures. Designs by Gustav Stickley include the bed, a Morris chair with its original leather upholstery, and a book rack with mortise-and-tenon structural details. The linen shades soften the room, and the rug and blankets in American Indian patterns enliven it.

92. The Strong house, San Diego, California. This house was designed by local architect Emmor Brooke Weaver (1876–1968), a relocated Iowan, whose work is characterized by its eloquent expressions of simple wood construction, and is also associated with the Arts and Crafts Movement. Clearly inspired by an Elizabethan cottage, it was constructed in 1905 for the William Hugh Strong family, and is still occupied by a family member. English influence is strong in its shingled roof made to resemble a thatched roof. There is half-timbering in the gable end. Adapted from the English Tudor style, the construction method uses real wooden structural elements to express its design, and they can be seen both inside and out. The glassed-in porch at right, enclosed in 1920, was once an open pergola. The interiors of the house feature dark beams and woodwork against light-colored walls, built-ins, and original insets of burlap in the dining-room wainscot. The building is sometimes referred to locally as the "Anne Hathaway House" or the "Elizabethan Cottage."

93. Bungalow in San Jose, California. The gable end of this house is a mélange of decorative half-timbering. Chiefly associated with the English Tudor style, half-timbering was originally a type of architectural process where the heavy timber structure would be infilled with "wattle and daub"— thin branches or wood laths—combined with mud or clay plastering to form solid walls. The recessed and arcaded porch, with its classical balustrade, suggests an Italian source rather than an English one.

94. Bungalow in Alameda, California. Fancifully shaped brackets march up and down the gable end of this shingled house, and are interspersed by three louvered attic vents. The diamond-shaped panes seen in the casement windows are often used to evoke an "Olde English" effect. Leaded diamond panes were used on seventeenth-century American homes in New England, and they may also appear in variations of the Colonial Revival style. Occupied by the same owners for almost fifty years, the house was first described to them as being a Craftsman cottage, a term they still prefer to bungalow.

95. Bungalow in Pasadena, California. The porch element of this house—in the form of a small tower—contributes to an appealing street presence. When constructed in 1922, its English-cottage style was much in vogue. The "jerkin-headed," or clipped gable ends are sometimes associated with thatched-roof designs. There was also a fashion for romanticized visions of English gardens in the Twenties, and this influence is seen in much of the landscaping design at the time. As focal points, gardens often included features like vine-covered archways, or arbors with built-in benches. Architectural trellis work, which by definition is designed as being integral to a building design rather than merely leaning against it, was related to this English garden influence. It was a rather inexpensive but effective way to get the maximum impact out of a modest house design, and was also a way to exaggerate its size.

96. "Urban bungalow" in San Francisco, California. Slipped into a narrow city lot, and sandwiched between two larger apartment buildings, this English-cottage-style bungalow retains a strong individual identity. High-density urban centers usually produce wall-to-wall townhouses, or even high-rise buildings to utilize scarce and expensive land in the most efficient way. For this reason, bungalows are much less common in older city areas, where narrow lot sizes tend to dictate building up rather than out. The curve of this street has created a wedge shape with a wide front, which has proven to be a convenient place for the tiny matching garage. Behind a patch of green and a towering evergreen tree, the distinctive lines of the "jerkin-headed" gable ends combine with the swelling roof above the porch to suggest thatching.

97. Bungalow court, San Diego, California. The range of styles that was used in bungalow courts is almost as diverse as those seen in larger family houses. Probably built in the Twenties, the Colonial Revival style of this court lends its vision of the all-American domestic ideal to this compound of little domiciles. The style is seen in the arch-topped porch roofs, traditional cornice moldings, narrow clapboard siding, and sidelight windows flanking the front door of each unit. The suggestion of individual front lawns, implied by the crossing concrete pathways, is a variation on the more typical common central garden space in such courts.

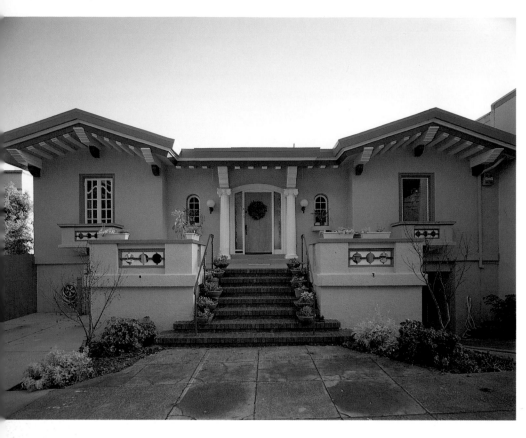

98. House in San Francisco, California. This 1915 building's eclectic design almost defies categorization. Because it is on a steep hillside, creating multiple lower levels in back, the house isn't a true bungalow. However, its single-story main living level, which originally included two small bedrooms, is of bungalow design. There was originally an open patio (now enclosed) in the rear, and the house formed a "U" shape around it. The lower levels in back have been developed for additional bedrooms and informal living areas. An elevated front terrace propels the house forward, and a rather grand brick stairway rolls out like the proverbial red carpet. Borrowed from the Colonial Revival style, a pair of classical Ionic columns frames the entry, which is further ornamented by sidelight windows and a shallow arch. A somewhat curious addition are the two large brackets above the columns, which extend upward to the eaves. These are repeated under the deeply projecting eaves of each gable. The stucco exterior and small arched top windows flanking the columns are reminiscent of the Spanish Colonial Revival. Other details show both French and Italianate influences. Perhaps this house can best be categorized as "Bungalow Free Style."

99. Irving Gill bungalow, San Diego, California. Almost suggesting an architectural topiary rather than a real building, this house in the Hillcrest area seems to exaggerate the concept of interrelating a structure to its landscape. Irving Gill (1870–1936) is recognized as one of the most significant California architects of the early-twentieth century. He built this house about 1905 and is believed to have lived here for a time. Gill's best-known work is in and around the San Diego area. Arriving here in 1893, he had come from Syracuse, New York, by way of Chicago where he worked with Adler and Sullivan for almost three years, during the time that Frank Lloyd Wright was still employed by that firm. His work is generally characterized by a strong, yet abstracted, influence of the Mission Revival style. In this façade, which suggests the flat front and curving roofline sometimes seen in the Mission Revival style, the arch form he favored is a major element. The compact floor plan is almost a "Z" in form, allowing courtyard-like side garden areas to bring light, air, and green outlooks to its interior that are surprising for a narrow city lot. A pioneering example of adaptive reuse since 1963, when it was first converted to an architectural office by Robert Ferris, the building continues as home to Ferris, Johnson & Perkins, an architectural practice that specializes in restoration projects, as well as nature-related interpretive centers. The house is listed on the San Diego City Historic Register.

100. Bungalow in San Diego, California. Defined by its elegantly arcaded porch, this 1920s house evokes the simplicity and atmosphere of the Mission Revival style. The use of arcading—the repetitive arches—together with the short, thick columns are forms adapted from the adobe construction of early California missions. The large curving brackets above the columns and the sinuous form of the attic vent dormer are other abstractions of the Mission Revival style.

101. Bungalow in Altadena, California. Glowing in the late afternoon sunshine, this house has many of the features that characterize the Spanish Colonial Revival style so typical of Southern California, such as the red tile roof, white stucco walls, and the archways. The house includes a small walled patio seen through the archway at the right. Most popular in the Twenties, this style is sometimes nicknamed "Hollywood Spanish" because of innumerable examples in and around that Mecca of popular culture. Florida also has many examples of this style.

102. The entrance gate to Casa de Pajaros, Pasadena, California. In a secluded site above the city, the graceful curves of this flagstone entry gate are a fitting introduction to the exceptional house behind it. The gate and house reveal a combination of architectural forms adapted from the Pueblo, Spanish Colonial, and Mission Revival styles. The house was constructed almost single-handedly by a relocated Pennsylvanian named Herman Koller. Beginning in 1928, the project became a kind of personal obsession, with building continuing into the mid-Forties, and involved Koller's endless scavenging for unique fragments of stone, wood, and tile that have been incorporated into the construction of the house.

103. Façade of Casa de Pajaros. Exceptional variety is achieved in the patterns and textures of the fascinating stone walls of this house, dated 1928. A true bungalow, its single-story room layout has an integral relationship with the landscape. There is an enclosed rear patio area, and several garden walls are inset with dull-glazed, low-relief pictorial ceramic tiles. The living room, which is behind the large arched window, features a high beamed ceiling and a large fireplace opposite the front door. The dining room is at the left.

104. Detail of the entryway of Casa de Pajaros. Note the handsome, heavy beams that support the ceiling of the porch.

105. Detail showing a tile set into the stone wall of Casa de Pajaros. This pictorial tile from the 1920s depicts an idealized scene at an old California mission. It is attributed to Batchelder. Such tiles, which were designed as decorative accents, are often found in fireplace surrounds and garden walls.

106. Detail showing a tile panel at Casa de Pajaros. Set into a rear porch wall, this is a "sampler" of fancifully designed low-relief tiles. Their matte-finish glaze was considered restrained and artistically appropriate for the home. The two tall side panels were probably designed to flank a fireplace opening, and all the tiles are attributed to Batchelder.

107. Detail showing a tile at Casa de Pajaros. The Arts and Crafts Movement has its light-hearted and whimsical side. This "leap-frog" tile is subtly colored and adorns a wall near a fish pond.

108. Detail of a bungalow porch, Alameda, California. There is an elephantine weight to these columns set on piers that look almost like Egyptian pylons. This boldness is characteristic of the Mission Revival style, which is sometimes prone to exaggerated scale. This house was constructed in 1913 by Strang Brothers, a local firm that built many bungalows in Alameda during this period, and it is part of an area that was designated as the Burbank-Portola Heritage Area in 1989.

109. Detail of a bungalow court, San Diego, California. A variation of the more typical plan of a central garden space ringed by individual units, this complex has a rather linear character. The design of this court is a mix of Spanish Colonial and Mission Revival influence, both fashionable styles when it was built in 1927. Each unit is a completely free-standing, self-sufficient dwelling, with a living room across the front, hardwood floors, french doors leading to the bedroom, and a kitchen with a breakfast nook and built-in ironing board. Bungalow courts were the forerunners of the motels of roadside America.

110. Bungalow in Piedmont, California. Seen in the late afternoon light of an autumn day, this stucco California Bungalow of the Twenties has a diagonally placed entry stair that utilizes the site to full advantage. The shaped parapet around the roof line and the flattened arches of the porch suggest a Mission Revival source. In contrast, the squared columns with their thick caps, and with miniature versions of the columns set above each, effectively combine with a chunky porch-roof overhang.

111. Bungalow in Palo Alto, California. This 1920s stucco house projects an elegance that is unusual for its small size. A recessed porch shelters triple french doors beyond a low railing wall, giving a strong horizontal feeling to the building that is emphasized by the handsome arched windows at the left, which retain their original wooden screens. The columns between the windows and the corbels are elegant details.

112. Bungalow, San Diego, California. An anomaly in its North Park neighborhood, this house with a "face-brick" skin over a wooden frame was built in 1924. A river-rock retaining wall makes an impressive entrance for the building that also has a matching foundation. The style of this bungalow appears to be a spare version of Mission Revival, as suggested by the arches and the curved parapet. It was built by a couple, living next door at the time. The wife was apparently from Michigan, and she missed its brick houses, which were conspicuously absent in California. So she convinced her husband to build this brick house.

113. Bungalow in San Jose, California. Startlingly modern when it was built, this Prairie-style house stands out from most of its neighbors in the Naglee Park area, as if it were newer than the others, even though it was probably constructed about the same time. Most of the houses in this area, developed between 1900 and the Twenties, reflect the various popular architectural styles of those years. The spatial sequence of this house comprises entering through a rather low-ceilinged space that leads to a dramatically higher one. Another feature of the Prairie style is the art glass that decorates the three clerestory windows that emphasize the striking height of the living room. The massive squared porch columns and deep overhangs of the strongly horizontal roofs also characterize the style.

114. Bungalow in Chico, California. Clearly articulated building forms, massed together to form a coherent and balanced composition, are hallmarks of the Prairie style at its best. Through a few bold strokes, this house achieves an asymmetrical balance, linked by aligning roof and window heights. The porch seems to be a complete entity, yet its roof appears to slice through the forms of the two higher masses behind it, and emerges again at the back of the building to tie the composition together. Its typical Prairie features include the shallow hipped roof and squared-off, cantilevered eaves, prominent chimney, and ground-hugging horizontality. In contrast, the square tapering porch columns, decorative brickwork accents, and repeating rectangular motifs around the face of the eaves are actually more Craftsman than Prairie style in character. There is a small open terrace at right, enclosed by low walls, whose square piers, with their brickwork detail, restate those of the porch.

115. Detail of figure 114 showing the decorative brickwork on the chimney and the handsomely framed windows.

116. Bungalow in Alameda, California. Although set in a development of closely spaced, modestly scaled bungalows of the Twenties, this house manages to spread generously in Prairie-style fashion, and its low profile makes it appear firmly rooted to its site. Not surprisingly, its sleek lines make many of its Craftsman-style neighbors appear old-fashioned in comparison. The very shallow hipped roof's deep, square-edged overhang and that of the front porch are expressed as two boldly overlapping horizontal planes. The asymmetrical grids of the original double-hung windows are another interesting feature of this house.

117. Bungalow in Alameda, California. The broad flattened shapes of the generous roof overhang, the porch columns, and the planters flanking the front steps show a strong Prairie-style influence. The severity of an all-white exterior allows only light and shadow to define its forms and textures, and almost presents a tropical, whitewashed appearance, underscored by the lush plantings. The possibility of a cozier interior is suggested by the unexpected touch of the original front door in a natural wood finish. Scaled for the smaller cars they were built for, the narrow side driveway and small detached garage in back are often seen in bungalow tracts.

118. The Austin house in Pasadena, California. This house was built by local contractors Grable and Austin. It is believed to have been John C. Austin's own residence, and he is the architect who in 1909 was credited with its design. This fascinating house appears to have been strongly influenced by traditional Japanese timber construction. The English-style diamond-paned windows seem a surprising addition to the rest of its design. The house has been substantially enlarged toward the rear by the current owners, who have made a close match to the original detailing. The Austin house has for some years been the subject of much scholarly controversy in terms of the sources of its design, and a near duplicate of the house is in Oakland, California.

119. Bungalow in San Diego, California. Overlooking a colorful Mediterranean garden that sprawls bountifully to the sidewalk, this 1910 house in the University Heights area has been occupied by various artists and promoters of the local opera for most of its life. Its design shows a combination of Oriental influence in the peaks of the gables, with otherwise mostly Craftsman-style forms and detailing. Working with local craftsman Larry Word, the owner recently designed and completed an addition to the back, and also added the Spanish-style peaked top to the rock chimney, which was inspired by one down the street. Large river-rock piers, matching those on the porch, support a pergola-covered porte-cochère over the driveway. Seen behind a blooming bougainvillea, the original front door has a natural-wood finish, beveled-glass panels, and typically oversized brass hardware.

120. Detail of a bungalow in Alameda, California. Looking something like a miniature temple from the Far East, the roof of the compact porch repeats the design of two main gables with upswept pagoda peaks, a style often seen in bungalows with an Oriental influence. In good repair, and still shining its original porch light, the house has a tiny attached garage (just out of view) that also sports a matching gable. This 1915 house was the first in its particular tract to be constructed by George Noble, a prominent Alameda developer, who was responsible for many of the bungalows built in this pleasant island community. Not as celebrated as their showier Victorian neighbors, such bungalows are worthy of greater notice and preservation.

121. The Black house, Pasadena, California. This corner property is a striking combination of Oriental and Craftsman styles. The partial second floor of this house contains the original three bedrooms and a bathroom. Several variations of the upswept pagoda shape are seen in the gable peaks, projecting double-curved roof beams, and the exotic turned-up forms of the porch columns. The house is located in the Pasadena Heights area, and was built by the Black family, who raised seven children here. The present occupants are the third owners, and upon purchase were given a copy of a page out of an unidentified plan book, which featured the design of this house. It stated that the cost to build "Plan No. 440" was $2,800. The cost of complete plans and specifications was listed as $10, or "Plans free if we build your home." According to Black family legend, the tapering open-frame porch columns, that look as if they might start rocking, were intended to be enclosed with wire and used as birdcages. The porch railing has the Oriental cloud-lift motif that is also seen in the work of Greene and Greene.

122. The Carr house, San Diego, California. This Oriental-Craftsman hybrid was designed and built in 1915 by builder/ contractor David Owen Dryden for George and Anna Carr in the North Park area. It is interesting to compare it to the house in Pasadena (fig. 121), a mirror image whose appearance, plan, and detailing are nearly identical. This house was the more expensive of the two (based on the plan-book price quoted for fig. 121), for its selling price was recorded as $6,550. Also on a corner site, its dramatic forms are heightened by contrasting paint colors. George Carr was employed by a local manufacturer of doors, windows, millwork, and art glass who did business with Dryden, and it is likely that such features in this house came from that company. The dining room features a built-in gumwood sideboard, very similar to one that appeared in Henry L. Wilson's 1910 *Bungalow Book*, featuring swags of metal chains attached to the wall at either side, which connect to the upper cabinet in a gesture of support. This house is sometimes referred to locally as the "Pagoda House of North Park," and has landscaping of appropriately Japanese inspiration.

# Related Arts and Crafts Homes
## "IN THE BUNGALOW TRADITION"

To keep the record straight, the houses included in this section should be referred to as Arts and Crafts houses, rather than as bungalows. These houses share many style traits (and even some planning features) of true bungalows, but since the original plans of their second floors included multiple bedrooms (rather than a partial second-floor attic space that was later converted) they are included here with the knowledge that they are not true bungalows. One outstanding exception to that qualification is the Lanterman House (figs. 128–131). Planned from its inception to have all of its bedrooms on the same floor as the main living spaces, it can therefore qualify as a true bungalow despite its large scale. (The whole area of its highly visible partial second floor is devoted to a ballroom.) Although the vast majority of true bungalows are modestly scaled houses, the Lanterman House serves to demonstrate that it is not necessarily size, but the house plan itself that defines a bungalow. What is most compelling about the other houses illustrated could be described as their "bungalow sensibility,"—the strong parallels that exist between these houses and true bungalows. On the inside, this is defined by a related sense of spatial organization, detailing, finishes, and furnishings. Moreover, it is primarily because of their interiors that these houses have been included here. They show an extraordinary range of Arts and Crafts features and furnishings, and can serve as inspiration for more modest bungalows. In many ways surprisingly similar, the architectural forms, proportions, and building materials seen on the exteriors of these houses foster some interesting comparisons to their modest counterparts.

123. David B. Gamble House, Pasadena, California. This landmark house was designed by two brothers, Charles Sumner Greene (1868–1957) and Henry Mather Greene (1870–1954), while practicing architecture as Greene and Greene. They came to Pasadena from Cincinnati, Ohio, in 1893. The house was built in 1908 as a retirement residence for David and Mary Gamble, whose family business was the Procter & Gamble company in Cincinnati. Described by Randell Makinson as one of the "ultimate bungalows," this house has come to epitomize all that one could hope to find in a bungalow on the grandest scale. Seldom has restraint been so luxurious. Photographed from a woodsy landscaped strip of land that shields the site from nearby traffic, this view shows the entire front elevation. Seen across an emerald-green lawn, the house has the wonderful patina of old wood. The sleeping porch on the right has a weightless quality that is firmly grounded by the rounded forms of a vine-covered retaining wall. It is with good reason that the influence of Japanese forms and sensibility is often cited in this and other Greene Brothers projects of this period. Yet the influence of Japanese style is more abstract than literal, and the skill and sensitivity with which it has been assimilated into the work of the Greenes is astonishing. Once the large scale of the house has been realized, it is somehow not overwhelming, for after almost nine decades the house has comfortably nestled into its site. It is a joy to see the roof lines of this great house silhouetted in a continuous sweep against the sky.

124. Detail of the entrance to the Gamble House. Glowing like amber against the dark shingled walls, the teak of the front entrance and windows has been crafted like a fine piece of furniture. Massive timbers are transformed into softly rounded shapes, hardwood is sculpted smoothly, and stained glass is mounted like jewelry. The main front door is exceptionally wide, and the sidelights that flank it are actually french doors that help provide maximum ventilation through the center of the house. The transom panels above the door have cloud-lift corners, and variations of the cloud-lift motif occur on other doors and windows elsewhere in the house. Using glass supplied by Tiffany Studios in New York, the stained-glass work was executed by Emile Lange, and it is—like the entire house—considered a masterpiece of the American Arts and Crafts Movement. The glass shimmers with iridescence when seen from the outside, and is almost beautiful enough so that one would never have to see the glass from the inside. Hanging from a beam that supports a projecting window seat in the second-floor stair hall, the lantern is discreetly emblazoned with the house number "4." Repair work around the small window at left has created a temporary contrast of new wood against the old. A grid of plain, square terra-cotta tiles set inside a banding of equally plain brick creates a practical flooring for the entry terrace.

(Overleaf) 125. Entry hall and staircase of the Gamble House. There is a hushed splendor of glowing wood and shadowy light in this extraordinary area, which bisects the house. Whether or not direct sun is reaching it, the stained glass of the entrance doors ignites the whole room. The stairway, with its undulating handrail that wraps around a built-in bench, suggests a wooden cascade. There are many small, dark, square wooden pegs set into the mahogany that always convey the sense of structure and are also important decorative details. On virtually every piece of wood, a waxy sheen and rounded edges invite one's touch. The lighting, hardware, and furnishings throughout the house were conceived by the Greenes as a single harmony. The walls and ceiling coffers are painted a creamy golden color that echoes highlights in the stained glass, and provides a muted contrast against the resplendent mahogany. The rugs are original furnishings, and the furniture made for this room is mostly out of view.

126. Living room of the Gamble House. The superb and spacious inglenook on the right reflects the same proportions as a wide bay window exactly opposite that faces the rear garden. The open beams above the inglenook support a pair of stained-glass lanterns that are suspended by leather straps. The living room is a much brighter area than the entry hall because of the large windows. There is direct access to a covered terrace through a glass door in the far corner. Suspended from the ceiling are three extraordinary stained-glass lighting fixtures. The entirely original furnishings include the custom-made rugs, which feature a stylized tree-of-life design, a popular Arts and Crafts motif. The caliber of the craftsmanship seen in the woodwork and built-ins is matched by that found in each piece of furniture. Nothing escaped the Greene's attention, least of all the superb upright piano at right, which is a good example of the level of marvelous detail to be found in their projects. Another example may be seen in the various stylized Oriental landscapes created in the hand-carved wooden frieze. The iron straps that clasp the beams at the right and the inset pegs that are scattered throughout the room as well as on the furniture, are actual structural devices.

127. Dining room of the Gamble House. Awash in a golden light reflected from the garden at the right, this room possesses warmth and intimacy that emanate from the beauty of the mahogany paneling, the furniture, and the splendor of the Oriental rug. Stained glass blazes above the built-in sideboard and in the door at the far-left corner that leads to the butler's pantry and kitchen. The dining-room's ceiling fixture is the most exceptional in the house. It is a brilliant integration of wood, glass, and joinery techniques. To the left of the fireplace, through a wide pocket door with stained-glass insets like those of the butler's pantry door, is the entrance hall. In a joint agreement with the University of Southern California, this great house was given by the Gamble family to the City of Pasadena in 1966. It has a regular schedule of visiting hours for public tours, and it is administered by the School of Architecture of the University of Southern California.

**128.** El Retiro, the Lanterman House, La Canada Flintridge, California. This house was built by Dr. Roy and Emily Lanterman, a Los Angeles physician and his wife, on land in the scenic La Canada Valley near Pasadena. This area was first developed by Roy's parents in the 1870s for housing and agriculture purposes. When the house was built in 1914, the Lantermans' two sons, Frank and Lloyd, were teenagers. After their parents died in the late Forties, the two unmarried brothers continued to live in the house, and kept the interiors, which had never been redecorated, unchanged. After their own deaths in the 1980s, the house was left to the City of La Canada Flintridge. Frank Lanterman's career as a State Assemblyman has encouraged the cause of preserving the house as a museum, and local volunteers have also set up a foundation to fund its maintenance and administration. Opened on a limited basis to the public in 1993, this enormous bungalow was constructed with reinforced concrete. In an area where these factors are major concerns, the structural and seismic strength, durability and resistance to fire of reinforced concrete were considered innovative. The exterior of the house has only recently been restored to its original appearance. The courtyard or patio plan of the house, showing the influence of early California haciendas, was adapted into a decidedly Craftsman-style design. The concrete-columned pergola, bracketing under the eaves, deep overhangs, and stone chimney all show connections to that style. The outdoor courtyard area, actually used for circulation between rooms not otherwise connected by corridors, is still missing its original fountain. The partial second floor is a capacious ballroom, which was mostly used by Mrs. Lanterman to stage local musical performances.

**129.** Detail of the decorative painting in the dining room of the Lanterman House. For this room, breaking out of the Craftsman style, Emily Lanterman chose a rather formal scheme of off-white woodwork combined with a hand-painted frieze of grapes and grape-leaf clusters, and with a band of scrollwork outlining the ceiling.

130. Detail of the living-room ceiling in the Lanterman House. A glance at the ceiling shows that this is no ordinary bungalow interior, for one is awestruck by the ornate handpainted borders outlining each ceiling coffer and the elaborate Renaissance-style frieze that encircles the room. The mottled texture of parchment-style glazing at the center of the coffers also appears on the walls. This is a huge room that is lit from the outside on all four sides, chiefly by multiple sets of french doors. This living room occupies the entire right wing of the house (fig. 128). All of the painted finishes in the building were recently cleaned and restored by Ed Pinson and Debrah Ware, of Pinson and Ware Painted Ornament.

131. Billiard room of the Lanterman House. With its geometric inlay suggesting the Viennese Secessionist style, the pool table converts to a billiard table. The beamed ceiling and painted ornament in the ceiling coffers echoes the living room. The tall-case clock is emblematic of the Colonial Revival style. The staircase, with a built-in seat at its base, leads to the ballroom. Note the lush foliage design in the frieze, similar to that in the living room.

132. Front door of the *Gray* house, Los Angeles, California. This 1909 house was designed by Pasadena architect Alfred Heineman, who began working with his brother Arthur, a building contractor, the same year this house was built. The Heinemans were responsible for many fine Arts and Crafts houses in the Los Angeles and Pasadena areas. The *Gray* house cost $8,600, considered an exorbitant price at the time. Not a bungalow, this full two-story house features a cantilevered front-door canopy, which is supported by a heavy chain that is visible above the center of the canopy. With cedar shingles used above, the first floor of the house is faced with a type of stucco called gunite. The front door enters directly into a forty-foot living room.

133. Living room of the *Gray* house. This room is brightly lit by many windows and a pair of french doors. The woodwork is believed to be made of Port Orford cedar. Proven to be resistant to marine parasites, this cedar became rare when the United States Navy purchased all the available groves. A tall Mission-style clock stands in the far corner, one of a number in the collection of the current owners. The ceiling is simply divided by shallow, wide beams, with pairs of light fixtures mounted directly onto them. The frieze area contains wide, wooden planks, which rely on grain and color for their ornamental value. The 1920s rug is one of a matching pair in the room, and is a machine-woven type that was very popular during that decade. Butterscotch-colored leather cushions on the oak seating and a collection of period textiles lend softness to the room. The owners, David Raposa and Ed Trosper, have an extensive collection of Mostique pottery by Roseville, such as the planter and its pedestal, as well as the vase and three bowls on the table at left, next to an oil-burning oak-base lamp with a trapezoidal stained-glass shade.

134. Dining room of the Gray house. The handsome procession of lights down the middle of this room were formerly outdoor fixtures at an East Los Angeles home of the same period. The built-in sideboard was recreated by the current owners from outlines left by the original. The column-like shapes with square "capitals" in its lower doors were repeated in the replaced swinging door to the kitchen at the right. Different paint colors help to define the high wood wainscot and frieze areas, and a wide molding is featured at the top of the walls. On the sideboard, there are two miniature Mission-style clocks at left, and several more pieces of Roseville Mostique pottery.

135. Sleeping porch at the Gray house. A commodious thirty-two feet in length, this room is enclosed with sliding windows, which replaced the original screens. The walls and ceiling are made of board-and-batten siding. Originally from a house in Oregon, the Old Hickory porch furniture comprises a matching suite. It includes a Morris-style chaise longue at right, and a long glider at the far end of the room. The maple floor replaced the original flooring of asphalt roofing material.

136. Entry of house in Angelino Heights, Los Angeles, California. A simple Craftsman design, this house was built in 1908 by the Joseph Garibaldi family, who had been in the state since the late 1850s. The present owners, Jim and Paula McHargue, purchased the house from the Garibaldi family in 1986. The house subsequently suffered a major fire, which destroyed its roof, and did extensive damage to the two floors below it. Miraculously, the original set of architectural plans and specifications, produced by the firm of Garrett and Bixby, survived the fire and made an authentic restoration possible. It was fortunate, also, that almost all of the original millwork, lighting fixtures, and hardware, especially on the first floor, could be carefully salvaged and restored. The success of the McHargues' efforts has since been officially recognized with an award from the California Preservation Foundation in 1991. Another coveted award came from the Los Angeles Conservancy in 1992. Perhaps most publicized was the receipt of two first prizes for both interior and exterior work from the National Trust for Historic Preservation's 1992 Great American Home Awards competition. The house was designed with a fully developed second floor that includes a roomy stairhall and three large bedrooms. The front door has its original brass hardware, which consists of a pair of oversized decorative hinges and a matching door handle.

137. Front hall of the McHargue house. The unusual staircase and the generous size of the front hall distinguish this house. Upon entering the hall, it is possible to see through the wide doorway of the living room at left into the dining room, for the doorway is framed by low walls. Each is topped at the right and left by squared columns, and lights hanging from the lintel above. Variations of this structural arrangement are seen in many bungalows, most typically between the living and dining rooms. Here, pocket doors open into the dining room. The unusual design of the staircase balustrade, with its rectangular cutouts, is similar to one published by Gustav Stickley in the November 1906 issue of *The Craftsman*. The upholstered settee at the foot of the stairs and the bookcase with leaded-glass panels are typical of the built-ins recommended by Stickley and seen in many houses of the Arts and Crafts period.

138. Dining room of the McHargue house. Electric bulbs are placed at the intersections of the box beams in the ceiling, for in 1908 bare filament-type light bulbs were regarded as sparklingly ornamental. At that time, many houses still relied on gaslight or, depending on location, perhaps used a combination of gas and electricity. The woodwork here is a thoughtful variation on the Craftsman style and has a good sense of scale. A bracketed plate rail aligns with the wainscot panels below, and is restated in the upper third of the built-in sideboard, which is flanked by tall pilasters. In the restoration, the woodwork throughout was stripped and stained, then given four coats of hand-rubbed shellac in order to achieve the present gleaming effect. The leaded-glass panels of the cupboards in the sideboard match those of the bookcase in the front hall. The beveled mirror at the back of the sideboard is a handsome source of reflected light for the room.

139. Tamaledge, the Evans house, Marin County, California. In this photograph taken about 1907, a local landmark is shown perched on its hillside ledge at the side of Mount Tamalpais. Long regarded by indigenous Indians as a sacred place, this towering mountain was the apparent inspiration for the house's name. It was built by Ernest and Letitia Evans, who had first planned to build on a lot they owned in Berkeley, and had already selected Bernard Maybeck to design their home. Meanwhile, after renting a house near here, they decided to build on this side of the bay instead. They also switched architects, and chose Louis Christian Mullgardt (1866–1942), a significant San Francisco Bay area architect. Although less celebrated than Maybeck, Mullgardt is best known for his residential commissions, many of which do not survive. Infusing Arts and Crafts design with subtle Asian references, his work has a strongly individual and sometimes bold character. The main entrance is flanked by a pair of monumental planters that are low-walled extensions of the house, and sprout from its battered walls like the paws of the Sphinx. The original plans called for a long, bridge-like pergola to connect the front door with an entry gate, thus spanning the hillside garden while visually securing the house to the ground. Although Mullgardt's ceremonial entry pergola was never built, years of maturing vegetation has helped the house grow closer to its site. More exposed in this early view, there is a particular clarity to the building's composition and to each material used. On the side of the building, three stepped windows reveal the location and angle of the staircase, which parallels the hillside.

140. Front entrance of the Evans house. A vintage climbing rose, one of several around the house, wreathes the front door and an original oversized stained-glass lantern. Several layers of wide, flat door casings lend a monumentality to the entrance, which is covered only by the deep eaves above the second story. The upstairs casement windows punctuate the deep horizontal band of the stucco.

141. Rear view of the Evans house. Spanning the full width of the house, the expansive enclosed porch adjoins the living and dining rooms. Above it, there is direct access from two bedrooms to an open deck formed by the porch's roof. The building's flaring base originally housed basement-level service areas. To the right, one of the entrance planters seen from the side shows how it is integrated into the main structure. Most of the exterior wood, including the clapboards, has been allowed to weather naturally, and the stucco of the upper level has remained unpainted. The diagonal braces that support the porch are not original, but were added to provide necessary support. Letitia Evans died in 1969. The house, fortunately, held many happy childhood memories for its new owner, Mrs. Evans's great-niece, who purchased it from the estate and has undertaken its major repair and restoration. Its continuous one- family ownership status has thus been preserved, along with a number of the original furnishings.

142. Front hall of the Evans house. The simple linear pattern of the leaded glass in the front door at the right is repeated in the square panels of the casement windows and elsewhere in the house. The floorlamp was designed by Mullgardt, who may have been hoping to design more of the furnishings for this project. The brick floor is laid in a herringbone pattern within a wide border of bricks set both parallel and perpendicular to the walls. A high wainscot of clearheart redwood (meaning that it is without knots or other imperfections) retains its original wax-only finish. Still in place is the frieze, made of a Liberty of London fabric that is woven in a stylized landscape pattern, a popular motif of the Arts and Crafts period. The ceiling panels retain their original embossed paper that is textured to resemble burlap and has a subtly reflective bronze-gold finish. Fragments of both materials, found stored in the attic when they were new, reveal that the fabric seen in the frieze is now much faded, while the ceiling paper is remarkably unchanged. The unusually graceful pair of wall sconces, their shades formed by separate glass panels delicately suspended to cover the light bulbs, are original to the house.

143. Detail of the staircase in the Evans house. The handsome staircase rises at one end of the living room, opposite the dining room, and the front hall is through a doorway to the left. A substantial newel post with columnar grooving supports an unusual balustrade of strong verticals and horizontals. The staircase is lit by three narrow ascending windows, which have glass leaded in the same linear design as the windows in the front hall.

144. Living room of the Evans house. At the heart of the house, this room flows easily into the adjacent areas, yet each area can be separated as needs dictate. Wide pocket doors open to the dining room beyond, while a wall of french doors behind the couch open to the porch and the beauty of the outside. Floor-to-ceiling redwood paneling forms a counterpoint to the strong horizontal rhythm of the ceiling's shallow beams, which are inset with panels of the same burlap-textured paper used in the front hall. The furniture in this room is mostly of the Craftsman style. The current owners have allowed the interiors to evolve from their near-original state, and have included a number of their own additions, such as the bronze Handel floorlamp, a 1920s painting by *Redbook* magazine illustrator Marshall Frantz, as well as a collection of richly colored Oriental rugs.

145. Detail of the living room in the Evans house. Dominating one side of the living room, built-in bookcases flank the oversized clinker-brick fireplace with its hand-hammered copper hood. The wall sconce is original, and the hand-wrought iron fireplace tools are especially attractive. The glow of the mica-shaded floorlamp reveals intact portière hardware above the pocket doors, and an oak Morris-style chair invites fireside reading and inspection of the many old books on the shelves.

146. Dining room of the Evans house. Four handsome built-in cabinets fronted with leaded glass flank a shallow bay of casement windows, containing glass that matches the windows in the stairwell. The high redwood wainscot and fabric frieze have been repeated from the front hall, and the ceiling duplicates that of the front hall and living room. The wall sconces are original, but the chandelier over the dining table is from the 1920s. The slant-top mahogany desk in the Queen Anne style is a fine example of Colonial Revival furniture of the turn of the century. To the left of the desk a door leads out to the porch, and to the right is a generous butler's pantry lined with its original glass-fronted cabinets, which leads to the kitchen.

147. Porch of the Evans house. High up in the treetops, this space merges inside with outside and epitomizes the casual appeal of the Craftsman style. Designed with decorative as well as functional properties in mind, the natural wood grids of the window sash and the beamed ceiling have acquired a softly aged patina. Access to the living room is through the multiple sets of french doors shown in figure 144. The dining room opens onto the opposite end of the porch. Window panels are also movable, allowing a virtually open-air space if desired. The slatted Craftsman-style oak porch swing and ceiling fixture are part of the original furnishings. At handrail height, linear wooden troughs were originally designed by Mullgardt to support planter boxes, but they also create a visual buffer against the precipitous drop to the hillside garden below.

148. Kitchen in the Evans house. This room's original character has been preserved intact, with its unpainted redwood walls and ceiling providing both texture and color. Pendant work lights of ribbed Holophane glass were added by the current owners to replace the previous single light bulb at the center of the room. This type of ribbed glass, first developed for industrial and laboratory area lighting, amplifies the effect of the light source. The commodious six-burner, double-oven stove, vented through the back of the living room fireplace, was a replacement in the 1920s of the 1907 original. The checkerboard pattern of the vinyl-tile floor approximates that of the earlier linoleum version.

149. Bathroom of the Evans house. This 1907 version of a state-of-the-art bathroom gleams with nickel-plated fittings, original porcelain-finish cast-iron fixtures, and practical built-in storage. Utilizing a split-bath arrangement, the toilet is located in a separate "water closet." This eases some of the problems of sharing a bathroom. The claw-footed sitz bath, at right, is fondly remembered by the current owner as handy for bathing young children and pets. Crisply enameled white woodwork reflects light from the corner windows. Black and white vinyl tiles are recent replacements. The original sunken tub is an unusual feature, with a shower at one end, and for contemplative soaking, restful outlooks into the trees.

150. The Randall house in Berkeley, California. Because of its clean lines and simplified detailing, the age of this 1909 house isn't immediately apparent. It was built for a civil engineer named Henry I. Randall. It has been documented that the cost of the lot was $3,450, and that the estimated building cost was about $4,000 (but the actual cost was probably higher). The unusually expensive land, in a desirable neighborhood near the University of California campus, also reflects an increased demand for land and housing on this side of the Bay, which occurred after the 1906 San Francisco earthquake. The house was designed by the local firm of Plowman and Thomas (George T. Plowman and John Hudson Thomas), who collaborated on about fifty houses in the Bay Area. Though it is not clear which of the two architects is more responsible for this design, it was Thomas (1875–1945) who is known to have corresponded most with the owners about design-related issues. Evoking a feeling of progressive English Arts and Crafts architecture, like that of C.F.A. Voysey, the hipped-roof structure at the left contains the living room. Massive corner buttresses provide a stylishly sturdy appearance. The prominence of this living-room wing serves to diminish the apparent size of the main house. The leaded-glass windows at the right, added when the recessed front porch was enclosed, now open into a small sitting room off the dining room. Originally, the stucco exterior was left unpainted, but the current trim color is close to that used for the trim in 1909. This austerely elegant house is enhanced by its well-tended plantings.

151. Living room of the Randall house. This room is contained in the front wing that is separate from the rest of the house (fig. 150). All of the woodwork is made of fir, which at that time was actually more expensive than redwood, and was also considered preferable by some for the more flexible staining and finishing effects it made possible. One enters the living room through a deliberately lowered ceiling that creates an alcove-like area, which houses a piano that is original to the house. Then the ceiling dramatically lifts, thus emphasizing the ceiling divisions, as well as the different sizes of the beams. A pair of facing built-in benches creates the feeling of an inglenook at the far end. The two largest pillows on the benches and the one on the Gustav Stickley "Morris" chair are period textile designs recreated by Dianne Ayers. The wall sconces are original, and have an unexpectedly asymmetrical placement. There is also a Gustav Stickley library table at the far windows. The feeling of a strong cross-axis in the central area is created by the bay window at the left and the fireplace opposite, which is dominated by a hefty full-width mantel.

152. Dining room of the Randall house. The large window that looks out on a lush grove of bamboo is flanked by built-in china cabinets on which is displayed a group of Arts and Crafts ceramics in greens and blues. A small sideboard by Gustav Stickley stands in front of the window with two of the Stickley dining chairs. The dining table is by Stickley Brothers. At the right is a small sitting room with panels of English stained glass. One of these leaded windows can be seen at the right of figure 150.

153. Stairway and upstairs hall of the Randall house. The design sophistication of the house is particularly apparent in this central area. Light streams through a screen-like wooden grid near the bottom of the staircase, an architectural detail that actually predates a similar one of 1916 by Charles Rennie Mackintosh, the great Scottish architect. The solidity of the posts and panels of the upstairs stair wall makes a fascinating contrast to the lightfilled screen wall below. At the far end of the hall is a closed built-in storage unit. The bookcase at the right was manufactured by Lifetime, and on top of it is a prototype ("breadboard") radio and speaker made by Atwater Kent around 1924. After such prototypes were mechanically perfected, cabinets would be designed to contain them.

154. House in Oakland, California. Although its neighbors are close by, this house has a feeling of privacy that is enchanced by the sheltering pines. The narrow lot made it necessary to situate all three bedrooms and the original bathroom on the second floor. Built in 1907 by the Piedmont Heights Building Company, the house remained in the same family until purchased by the current owners, David and Jackie Allswang, in 1969. Helped by the fact that it had never changed hands, few significant changes had been made inside or out. A sheltered spot for an Adirondack-style chair, the recessed porch is contained within the overall lines of the roof. The windows at right belong to the library alcove, and the large dormer contains the master bedroom.

155. (*Above*) Living room of the Allswang house. The rather modest exterior of this house doesn't hint at the well-developed sequence of spaces within. A partial screen wall of vertical wood slats hides the entry area, which extends behind the clinker-brick fireplace. Across the living room ceiling a grid of beams reaches into the entry area, and at each intersection hangs an original light fixture of textured amber glass and hammered copper. This view is from the doorway opening into the dining room, with the library alcove visible at the left. The arrangement of squared columns on low walls flanking these open doorways is often seen, and helps the house plan to achieve a successful flow between living spaces. The green ceramic umbrella stand holding a cane collection is a Weller piece, and the pottery collection on the fireplace features pieces in the Roseville Sunflower pattern. The small oak rocker is by Gustav Stickley, and the bentwood rocker, manufactured by the Kohn Company of Vienna, Austria, dates from around 1900. A small English Arts and Crafts copper fireplace screen sits on the hearth.

156. (*Opposite, top*) Library alcove of the Allswang house. This open-alcove room displays an English Arts and Crafts wallpaper frieze created by the famous English designer Walter Crane (1845–1915). First shown at the 1900 Paris Exposition, this is a modern reproduction by Bradbury and Bradbury. This ornamental Lion and Dove frieze features the words "The wilderness shall blossom as the rose," on an undulating ribbon, which entwines a lion and a white dove, all set against a rambling rose. The leather Morris-style chair at left, dating from about 1910, was made in Cincinnati by The Shop of the Crafters. It is unusual for an American Arts and Crafts piece to be decorated with inlay work of this type, which is similar to Viennese Secessionist design motifs, but the inlay was characteristic of this shop. On the Japanese tansu chest at right is a small copper boudoir lamp with a mica shade by Dirk Van Erp, a famous master metalsmith of the Arts and Crafts period. The alcove is flanked by built-in bookcases, and a window seat spans the full width between them. On the desk is a copper and mica lamp recently crafted by Michael Adams of Aurora Studios. The period desk was made by the Cadillac Desk Company of Grand Rapids, Michigan. A hinged writing surface is built into the center drawer, allowing it to be used as both a desk and a library table, with open shelves at the sides.

157. (*Opposite, bottom*) Dining room of the Allswang house. The glass-fronted cabinets of the built-in sideboard contain a fine collection of Arts and Crafts pottery. Displayed on the plate rail are Royal Doulton plates in the Poppy pattern in two different color schemes. The oak slatback dining chairs are reminiscent of work by the English designers C.F.A. Voysey and Arthur H. Mackmurdo. The sideboard at left was made by Charles Stickley, and on it is a pottery collection of the Roseville Vintage pattern, so named because of the stylized grape-and-vine motif. In perfect working order, the oak-horned Victrola at the right, manufactured by the Victor Company about 1905, provides appropriate period music.

118

158. House in Alameda, California. Constructed by local builders Delanoy and Rantlet in 1912, this house was occupied from the late Teens until 1984 by the Wallin family, when it was purchased by the current owners. A thorough restoration followed. Much of the work was done by the new owners, and included replacement of all the building's mechanical systems, the foundation, and roof. They also reshingled the second floor level and had the original windows duplicated. The overall design of the façade is a fine example of architectural interest achieved with contrasting materials and textures. The restored stucco on the walls of the first floor is unpainted. Brick is used as a facing for the foundation and for the pilasters that frame a recessed entrance porch, which is further defined by the deep shadows enclosed in the strong brick archway. The handsome arch is restated in the curving brick border of the front lawn, which is part of a recent landscaping scheme to enhance the house. Using an appliquéd Arts and Crafts-style tulip motif, which was copied from the leaded and beveled-glass pocket doors inside (see fig. 160), the tailored curtain panels were made by the owners.

159. Front hall of the Alameda house. Offering a spacious welcome, this area is characterized by the spare directness that is so typical of many Arts and Crafts interiors. Note the extra-wide front door, the very wide window at the left, the sturdy simplicity of the staircase, and the built-in bench just visible at the lower left. The massive oak tall-case hall clock suggests the influence of C.F.A. Voysey in its overall form and hardware, and that of Charles Rennie Mackintosh in the design of the stained-glass door panel. The ceiling light is made with metal designs silhouetted against pale stained glass. The Roseville jardiniere and stand are in the Mostique pattern.

160. Dining room of the Alameda house. The source of the tulip motif that was used in the design of the fabric panels hanging in the front living-room windows (fig. 158) is seen at the center of each of the beveled-glass pocket doors. This set of doors divides the living and dining room, and another set, opposite the dining-room windows, leads to a small den used as a family room. The woodwork is familiar: massive box beams, a high wainscot, and at left, a long window seat. The commodious built-in sideboard has clear glass panels on its upper cabinets. Under the cabinets are panels of original crinkled or crazed glass, each being framed with clear mirror glass. The owners built the large dining table, which is patterned after a Gustav Stickley design, and the dining chairs, with a curved crest rail, were made by L. & J.G. Stickley. Using a ginko-leaf design by Gustav Stickley, the table runner was adapted and embroidered by the owner's daughter.

161. Kitchen of the Alameda house. The owners, professional builders and restorers of pipe organs, found a number of their skills helpful in realizing the kitchen of their dreams. Assembled as a new interpretation of period forms, this design is entirely their own creation. The form of the upper cabinets is based on the design of a Gustav Stickley glass-fronted bookcase, and was adapted for use as wall-mounted kitchen cabinets. To achieve the finish on the woodwork, all of the quarter-sawn oak cabinets were "fumed" with ammonia, a process in which the tannic acid present in the oak reacts to ammonia fumes in a sealed area, giving the wood a ripened or aged quality. The maple floor is decorated with butterfly-shaped "keys" of inlaid walnut similar to a design Stickley presented in the October 1905 issue of *The Craftsman*. Stickley's designs were also the inspiration for the hammered-copper hood over the stove, as well as for the antiqued-copper drawer and cabinet pulls. Out of view at the left is the front of the refrigerator, which was faced with wood in a design adapted from a Stickley folding screen. The countertops are made of gray granite.

162. In the family room of the Alameda house. Centered on a small Craftsman-style oak side table, a Handel lamp, with a delicately colored stained-glass shade, illuminates the red tones of the fir wainscoting. The family room opens into the dining room through pocket doors with beveled-glass panels that match those seen in figure 160.

163. Front entrance of a house in Berkeley, California. Massive wooden brackets convey a sense of importance to the recessed front door. Window boxes generously spill flowers and ivy over a recently reshingled façade. This inviting house was built in 1905 and designed by San Francisco architect Albert Schroepfer for a relative named Lawrence Schroepfer. The unusual front door displays a strongly figured grain and is studded decoratively with butterfly-shaped "key" inlays. Arboreal highlights of the property include a Grey cedar brought here from Canada, and a Sequoia that is now six feet in diameter. From 1908 to 1941 the house was owned by a leading stained-glass artisan named Harry Hopps, who used the upstairs bedrooms as his production workshop for a time. The present owners rescued the house from a state of neglect, and have restored it to pristine condition.

164. Living room of the Berkeley house. This cheerful room opens to the front hall and to the dining room on the right. The room is paneled in redwood, and above the mantel of the tiled fireplace are three inset panels of mirror lit by a pair of period brass wall sconces. To the right and left of the fireplace is a pair of window seats and narrow built-in bookcases. A reproduction of a period Liberty of London fabric has been used for the casement-window curtains. Embroidered pillows by Dianne Ayres soften the corners of the window seats and the large oak settle at the right. Another recent Arts and Crafts design is the floor lamp by Sue Johnson. Still retaining their original leather upholstery, a set of Craftsman furniture includes the rocker at the left, the armchair opposite, and the small settle under the far window.

165. (*Opposite*) Dining room of the Berkeley house. The current owners have sensitively replaced in period style parts of the house that were lost in a fire a number of years ago. Based on their observations of similar local interiors and their diligent perusal of resource material, they designed the capacious built-in china cabinets and central sideboard. Because of its irregular, rippled effect, glass salvaged from the old replaced windows was used on the fronts of the cabinets. Wood moldings carried around the room outline the Maytree frieze, a classic English Arts and Crafts design by Walter Crane, which has been reproduced by Victorian Collectibles and installed here by Gary Yuschalk and Larkin Mayo of Victorian Interiors. Executed by Woody Vermeire, the walls below the frieze have been glazed in a soft green. Multiple sets of french doors lead to a covered wraparound deck, where one can hear the gentle sound of the stream below and view the park-like garden.

166. (*Below*) Kitchen of the Berkeley house. Once the victim of an incongruous remodeling in the 1950s, the low-key restraint of this room's renovation has successfully achieved the owners' goal of creating a modern working kitchen with an Arts and Crafts sensibility. Planning every detail, they based their work on observations of other old-house kitchens that hadn't been drastically altered. The handsome cabinets are made of Douglas fir trimmed in redwood and were stained to give them a feeling of age. The Wedgewood stove from the 1920s is an exception to the priority given to the concealment of modern appliances. A wood-faced refrigerator at the left matches the cabinets. A similarly disguised dishwasher is housed in the central work island with the butcher-block top. Period reproduction hardware is used throughout, and lighting fixtures were assembled from antique parts, using square Holophane glass shades. The sink area is beautifully illuminated and ventilated by a broad band of casement windows. This view of the kitchen has been taken from the open breakfast area, which also has french doors leading to the covered deck.

167. (*Above*) House in Piedmont, California. Sheltered beneath the sweeping reaches of its enormous roof, with its multiple levels of clinker-brick stairs, landings, and a massive foundation, this house seems to grow out of its gentle hillside. Possessing on a grand scale much of the intimate charm of a bungalow, the generous lot and sculpted landscaping shows the house off to its best advantage. There is a possible influence of Greene and Greene, whose nearby work is the Thorsen house of 1908 in Berkeley, for both buildings share a similar siting and an extravagant use of brick to anchor them to the ground. Other similarities include massive projecting roof beams and rafters, and a deliberate rounding of the edges of these exposed structural elements. The strong composition of the façade strikes an asymmetrical balance between its bold projecting gable peaks and the horizontality of two railing-topped projections with oversized square rafter tails. Set into the shingled surface of the building, and also echoing the work of Greene and Greene, are several windows that show variations of the cloud-lift motif.

168. (*Opposite*) Detail of entrance porch. A closer look at this handsomely detailed house shows the architect's skillful blending of materials and their textures. The massive wooden timbers, softened by their rounded edges, project from the eaves with their size varied according to their structural importance. The flooring uses simple terra-cotta pavers, set flush with a surrounding brick border. The brick on this house is more refined than the usual clinker brick, and appears to have been chosen more for its mottled coloring than for any extremes of texture. Pierced by vertical openings, the substantial low brick walls of the porch form its railings. Softly complementing the gray-blue of the window sash, with its Oriental cloud-lift cross bars, is the warm subtlety of the natural-color palette found in the brick, terra cotta, shingles, and timber work.

# Classic Upgrades
## OLD HOUSES WITH NEW WORK OF QUALITY

With a focus on interiors, the following group of houses includes some original, intact rooms; some that have been restored to their original condition; and others that are best described as renovations—newly conceived work in an old house. It is in these renovated interiors that a number of imaginative and appropriate new ideas are spotlighted, which will be of particular interest and use to those presently contemplating changes in their bungalows or in larger Arts and Crafts houses. Although other types of recent work on old houses have been illustrated and dis-

cussed in previous chapters, this section specifically features renovation projects. While it is hoped that this book will encourage the preservation of historic interiors that survive intact, it is also hoped that when they haven't, sympathetic renovations will be done in a similar spirit as those shown here. An old house can offer a lot of information, even if it has been greatly changed, so it is advisable to try to "listen" to what the house has to say before proceeding to change it further. It is also a good idea to get some professional design help from a qualified source.

169. Detail of the front hall of a house in the Windsor Square district, Los Angeles, California. The design of this gracious Arts and Crafts house, built in 1912, is attributed to the well-known Pasadena architect, Alfred Heineman, and has a number of features associated with his work. Also notable is the fact that it was the first Los Angeles residence of famed humorist, actor, and author Will Rogers (1879–1935). The current owners, film director Scott D. Goldstein and his wife, set decorator Lauren Gabor, have sensitively underlined the early-twentieth century character of the house with a range of finishes and details appropriate to the period. At the left is one of the sidelights that flank the front door, and which open for additional ventilation. The wainscoting and crown molding are of matching quarter-sawn oak. The geometric forms in the leaded art-glass panel of the sidelight reflect the gable design of the house façade, and were an inspiration for the motifs used in the frieze. These stencil designs, and the others seen in the house, were adapted by Goldstein and executed by Pinson and Ware Painted Ornament. The geometric motif used in the handmade copper-and-mica wall sconces is repeated in the copper hardware and used on the doors throughout the house. This fixture, and the other lighting in the house, was designed by Goldstein, and crafted by Tony Smith of Buffalo Studios.

170. Sunken den/library of the Windsor Square house. Pocket doors part to reveal this view of an intact period room: finishes, furnishings, and decorative objects form an overall harmony. Although axially aligned with the living room, this room is set apart by a change in floor level and woodwork. The unusually extensive use of feather-grain mahogany continues in the ceiling, where it is used for both beams and panels. The rich natural color and luminous grain of these surfaces are beautifully lit by a copper-and-art-glass ceiling fixture with a flaring top. This form is repeated in matching wall sconces above the fireplace. A band of casement windows admits diffused light at the left, and a pair of original leaded art-glass windows on the fireplace wall depict Southern California landscapes. For example, the window on the right shows a mission with nearby Mount Baldy in the background. The geometric designs of the art-glass fronts of the bookcases flanking the fireplace are repeated in the pocket doors, which are out of view. The fireplace is faced with original olive-brown tiles manufactured by the Los Angeles Tile Company, and a harmoniously colored and specially glazed grasscloth wallcovering replicates a period treatment.

171. Detail of the dining room of the Windsor Square house. This doorway leading to the front hall is hung with portières, a feature typical of the period that is usually excluded from the Arts and Crafts homes of today. Designed by Scott Goldstein, the portières have bandings and corner block motifs in a soft rust appliquéd on contrasting gray-green linen, and executed by Dianne Ayres. The gray-green of the portières is repeated in the floral-stenciled design of the frieze.

172. Back hall of the Windsor Square house. Aligned with the front hall, this access to the rear garden provides good cross ventilation through the french doors. Visible outside to the right is a wisteria-covered pergola of redwood. The woodwork in this room is made of fir and redwood. The wainscot panels are inset with natural-colored burlap, a characteristic period treatment that emphasizes texture. Acknowledging the room's connection to the garden, the frieze is stenciled with a floral design that includes a Glasgow Rose inspired by the work of Roycroft designer Dard Hunter.

173. Dining room of a house in San Francisco, California. This room is in a grand 1912 house designed by architect Edward F. Young for a former mayor of San Francisco, and it has been sensitively renovated by its current owners. Realizing that the home's original woodwork had been carefully preserved, they commissioned a decorative scheme for the dining room that would appear as if it were original. Like many imposing homes of the period, this one features many Arts and Crafts elements created in a very refined style. There is a high oak wainscot capped by a plate rail. Pocket doors with arching beveled-glass panels lead to the front hall. An oak mantel shelf and panel behind it are set into a fireplace faced with softly mottled tiles. At the right and left, the design of the shelf and its supporting bracket are repeated in the tops of the two built-in china cabinets. With beveled-mirror panels at the back, the cabinet tops also function as sideboards, and their leaded-glass cabinet doors have an Art Nouveau feeling. The ornate gilded ceiling fixture and wall sconces are original. The mahogany dining set contributes a Colonial Revival accent. Above the fireplace is a single panel of Walter Crane's 1900 Lion and Dove wallpaper pattern, reproduced by Bradbury & Bradbury. Continuing in that English Arts and Crafts style is the frieze that is covered in a reissued 1906 Lincrusta pattern. Its repeating Tree of Life, a popular Arts and Crafts motif, is linked by a ribbon and the Art Nouveau whiplash curves of its entwining tree roots. The raised relief of the frieze is emphasized by several painted finishes: a background of wood graining to match the adjacent oak, gilded trees to suggest metalwork, and accents of deep red and blue-green to resemble tooled leather. The heavily embossed Anaglypta ceiling paper, another reissued period design, has been softly glazed to resemble antique plaster work. Joni Monnich executed all of the painted finishes, and Peter Bridgman installed the various wallcoverings used on the fireplace, frieze, and ceiling areas. Paul Duchscherer was responsible for the room's design concept and its coordination through Bradbury & Bradbury's Design Service.

174. Bungalow in San Leandro, California. This exceptional design of 1915 commands the attention of even the most casual bungalow watchers. It was built by an affluent San Francisco couple as a weekend retreat and vacation house. At that time, this area was rural and largely covered with cherry orchards. The house stayed under the same ownership until the surviving widow died in 1971 and left it to their gardener of twenty years. It was acquired by the present owners in 1991. A house that is a near twin to this one is in nearby Alameda, so it is probable that both came from a bungalow plan book. The bold forms of its multiple crossing gables, huge brackets, flower boxes, and sheltering eaves, serve to make this house appear larger than it is. Decoratively shaped rafter tails and bargeboard ends further extend the reaches of the roofline. The diagonally placed front door emphasizes the corner location of the house, and helps create two distinct porch areas. Oversized river-rock piers anchor the airy porch structure, which may also be reached from the dining room through narrow french doors. This house is rich with period art glass. Generally set in narrow horizontal panels above other windows, the imagery includes a stylized landscape to the right of the front door, and a flight of life-sized swallows in the gable at the far right.

175. Living room of the bungalow in San Leandro. The open floor plan of this handsome room leads to the dining room, at the right, behind the leaded-glass pocket doors with their square accents of green glass. Through the arched opening at the far end of the room one spies the art glass and built-ins of the library/study alcove. However, what really stuns the eye is the extraordinary fireplace wall of pale concrete brick that stretches almost the full length of the room. The arched fireplace opening is set between two similar ones, each having art-glass doors that enclose bookcases. The tapering chimney breast contains a Gothic-style opening that is electrically backlit to illuminate an original art-glass panel of an owl in a tree silhouetted against a full moon. Reddish-stained fir woodwork is used in a box-beamed ceiling of complex design. The original ceiling fixture resembles those seen in early movie palaces. The light from inside its lower section is reflected off the light-colored concave facets of its middle part. The richly patterned Bradbury & Bradbury wallpaper frieze helps to draw together the diverse elements of the room. At the left, new interpretations of Arts and Crafts design are seen in the reading chair and matching stool of cherry, designed and built by Debey Zito Fine Furniture. The smooth, spare lines of the chair feature on both sides copper insets in the form of flying birds.

176. Study/Library alcove of the bungalow in San Leandro. Facing south and west, this charming room always has ample light to bring to life the art-glass landscapes that make this room such a delight to be in. The open archway into the living room and the space-saving built-ins help this compact area to feel more spacious. The bench, softened by pillows with Arts and Crafts designs adapted by Dianne Ayres, wraps around a corner at the right. The bookcase, with its gridded-glass doors, faces a drop-front desk with multiple cubbyholes. The reddish wood tones and brilliant colors of the art glass are echoed in a frieze of floral and geometric wallpaper by Bradbury & Bradbury, which was created from period pattern and border designs. The small occasional table by the bench and the side chair at the desk were designed and crafted in cherry by Debey Zito. The wallpaper design coordination was by Paul Duchscherer, and its installation.throughout was by Peter Bridgman.

177. (*Opposite*) Detail of the dining room of the bungalow in San Leandro. This room retains all of its original features. The grape-and-vine motif of the art glass and the frieze was considered an appropriate theme for dining rooms. Intended to approximate the effect of hand-tooled leather, the embossed-paper frieze incorporates reflective metallic inks in gold, silver, and other colors. In the art-glass panels above the windows, a flamboyant butterfly motif that recalls the Art Nouveau style is combined with the grapes (and, for some unknown reason, the panel at the right was installed upside down). The box-beamed ceiling is similar in design to the one in the living room, and is also made entirely of wood. A collection of whimsical teapots is visible behind the tulip motifs of the art-glass panels. The side chair, by Debey Zito, is part of a matching cherry dining set.

178. Detail of a bungalow porch in Pasadena, California. An exercise in stylish restraint, this porch offers a pleasing combination of horizontals and verticals. Situated not far from the Arroyo Seco, the house was first constructed on a different side of the same block, moved to its present site in 1918, and then enlarged. Although the main living level is one story, the sloping site of its final location allowed a large basement to be added. Stained-glass lanterns of the period light the way to the front door, and the dining room at left casts a golden sheen through the screens of its three french doors. Still surviving on the front door, the period hardware has acquired a subtle patina. The current owners embarked on a major renovation of the interior in 1990 under the direction of architect Timothy Anderson, who is now relocated in Seattle, Washington.

179. Kitchen of the bungalow in Pasadena. This spacious room was created from the space occupied by the original kitchen, pantry, maid's room, and bath. There is still a large separate pantry area with a second sink and dishwasher. The entrance to the dining room is at the right of the imposing, reconditioned 1930s Magic Chef stove. The embroidered curtains are based on a Gustav Stickley design of ginko leaves adapted by Dianne Ayres.

135

180. Living room of the bungalow in Pasadena. Formerly hidden by a low, flat ceiling, the shallow peak of the roof was exposed during the renovation of the expansive living room. Through the left window of the pair above the fireplace, the original massive river-rock chimney is now visible. These windows were added to admit additional natural light into the height of the room. Matching the chimney's river rock, a reconstructed fireplace was enlarged to be in scale with the room's new proportions. Although the ceiling has been lifted, the ground-hugging feeling of the bungalow roof has been happily preserved, and the room still feels predominantly horizontal. Wrapped around the far corner, a band of casement windows and their windowseat offer pleasant views of both the inside and outside. A collection of Arts and Crafts period furniture is supplemented by a deeply-cushioned leather sofa and lounge chair, and the whole is accented by the color and geometric patterns of American Indian rugs. The copper and mica wall sconces were recently crafted by Tony Smith of Buffalo Studios.

181. Detail of the dining room in the Howell (Doolittle) house, Altadena, California. This 1912 house was designed and built by Harold Doolittle for George and Susan Howell, local patrons of the arts, and it is believed to be the only house he designed. A mechanical engineer by profession, his diverse artistic talents extended to furniture design, photography, film, and print-making. The current owner, artist and muralist Lynne McDaniel, has created the dining-room's extraordinary frieze, which is in the style of California's early twentieth-century "plein air" painters. This style of painting outdoors is associated with the California Arts and Crafts Movement, and was contemporary with it. The continuous landscape of this frieze encompasses an ever-changing panorama that seems to continue behind the door and window openings and the handsome built-in china cabinet at the right.

182. Detail of a bedroom in the Doolittle house. Lynne McDaniel is fortunate to have a visual history of her house. The original owners compiled an album of about eighty photographs that also included descriptions of color schemes, materials, and some wallpaper samples. Also surviving are the original house plans, which now form a framed procession around the library. In one of the old photographs of this bedroom, enough of a former wallpaper frieze was visible to enable it to be recreated as the stencil pattern seen here. Bedrooms of the Arts and Crafts period typically had pale color schemes, usually with woodwork painted a light color and combined with a floral wallpaper or stencil motif. On this wall, the frieze of stylized roses and wisteria has been stenciled over a base of soft yellow that was sponged to achieve its softly mottled texture. The upper wall and ceiling are painted the palest shade of sky blue. McDaniel also did the two small "plein air" paintings on the left wall.

183. Front entrance of a house in the San Francisco Bay Area. The crisp, smooth angularity of this entryway seems almost an abstraction of the Craftsman style. Constructed about 1912, the original two-story house has been used since the 1950s as two units, thus the reason for the two front doors. In 1989–1990, the house was given an extensive renovation under architect William P. Coburn, which included the addition of an interior staircase near the back, and a study/bedroom beyond it. Both of the previous front doors were replaced by oak doors in the Craftsman style, and built by Louis Kern.

184. Rear stairwell of the house in the San Francisco Bay Area. These newly constructed stairs have been designed to give the impression that they are original to the house. A group of Lincrusta panels with a Tree of Life motif were installed by Peter Bridgman to ascend the staircase in the form of a stepped wainscot. The panels were grained by Joni Monnich to resemble oak, so their pattern is somewhat subdued, and their design is revealed by reflected light. Lincrusta is a practical wainscot choice for walls subject to wear and abuse, and is also suitable for hallways and dining rooms. Above the wainscot is wallpaper in a foliage design adapted from a William Morris pattern by Bradbury & Bradbury. Small windows in the stairwell assure that it is flooded by daylight. Through Bradbury & Bradbury's Design Service, Paul Duchscherer was consulted for the project's various wallcovering schemes.

185. Detail of the living room of the house in the San Francisco Bay Area. Requiring a major reconstruction during the renovation, the original buff cast-stone blocks of the fireplace have acquired a wide variety of textures. The woodwork of this room duplicates remnants of the original, and the wallpaper frieze is a Bradbury & Bradbury adaptation of a William Morris design. Handcrafted metalwork is represented by the bucket for wood on the hearth and the copper bookends visible in the open sides of the bookcase.

186. Detail of the study/bedroom of a house in the San Francisco Bay Area. This room's period ambiance successfully creates the feeling of an Arts and Crafts room within a newly constructed addition. The redwood millwork, including a board-and-batten wainscot, contributes its distinctive color variations. Architect William Coburn designed the wall sconce, which was crafted by Marvin Metal. Above it, wallpaper in the William Morris Marigold pattern has a stencil-like border with a Tudor Rose motif, both adapted by Bradbury & Bradbury. The custom-made curtain designs and an embroidered pillow cover (both by Dianne Ayres) restate the grape-and-vine motif of the art glass above, which was executed by Bruce St. John Maher. Its design includes a scroll, inscribed with a quotation from the prologue to Chaucer's *The Legend of Good Women*, in which the poet describes the garments of the God of Love: "In with a fret of rede rose-leves / The fresshest syn the world was first bygonne." It is characteristic of English Arts and Crafts design to draw on medieval sources, which served to inspire such thematic decorative schemes.

187. Dining room of a house in the San Francisco Bay Area. Aglow in the afternoon light, this room's pleasing proportions are readily apparent. As was necessary in the living room, the period-style woodwork had to be mostly recreated. The box beams seem to push out the bay window, and a rhythmic frieze of irises and bulrushes, adapted by Bradbury & Bradbury from a Walter Crane design, serves to link the windows and doors above the wood wainscot. There is an unusual oak oil lamp on the sideboard, and the other lighting fixtures are also of the period. The concept of stylishly crossed table scarves, here embroidered in a Gustav Stickley design adapted by Dianne Ayres, was illustrated in the November 1905 issue of *The Craftsman* magazine.

# New Construction
## THE ARTS AND CRAFTS STYLE IN EVOLUTION

In the realm of contemporary architecture and interior design, the Arts and Crafts style has a promising future. Many of the same qualities that drew people to it in the early years of this century are still attracting them now. With an exceptionally broad appeal even to those who prefer to live in new houses or with new furnishings, its straightforward design approach and the use of natural materials have proven to be a timeless combination. The photographs that follow are a brief sampling of the kind of work that is being created today in the various evolving versions of a new Arts and Crafts style. Just as it was true in the beginning, it is readily apparent in these examples that the style allows for a wide margin of creative inter-

pretation on the part of the architect, designer, or craftsperson. Especially in the previous chapter and also throughout this book, other examples of high-quality contemporary work in this style have appeared in period settings, and often alongside period furnishings. As the Arts and Crafts Revival style seems to be just reaching its stride, this is indeed a promising state of affairs. Inasmuch as the Arts and Crafts Movement inaugurated the practical sensibilities that have characterized much of twentieth-century design, it would appear that the Craftsman style will continue to flourish and endure well into the twenty-first century, and beyond.

188. New house in St. Helena, California. Many of the architectural details seen on Craftsman-style bungalows and other related houses of the period are restated in this new design. There are exposed roof-beam ends in the gables, and rafter tails peeking from beneath the deep eaves. Other familiar features include short, tapering columns set upon square shingled piers connected by low railing walls, and groupings of casement windows set off by smaller panes at their tops. This two-story Arts and Crafts-style house, constructed on a narrow lot, also makes the most of the high visibility created by its corner siting. By keeping the higher building mass toward the rear, it allows the distance necessary to permit a horizontal sweep of the low, peaked roofline to extend out to a covered porch area at the left. The front door is sheltered by an abbreviated version of the same roofline, which creates the entry porch at the right. Connecting these two porch areas is a long pergola, which permits greater amounts of direct sunlight to reach the building's windows. It also serves to expand the usable space of the porch areas, as well as the apparent size of the house. Visible here is the linear interest of shadow lines, cast by the pergola's crossbeams, over the building's shingled surface. The siting is blessed by the close proximity of a mature redwood tree, a "borrowed landscape" to enjoy for free.

189. Detail of a rustic staircase at Mariposa, Hollywood, California (figs. 84–91). Designed and built by "rustic constructivist" Atli Arason, this stairway ascends to a scenic walking trail, which leads up and around an unspoiled mountain canyon. The site has an uncanny sense of separation from the nearby environment. It is one of several handcrafted wooden structures that dot the secluded site, and form pleasant punctuations in the landscape. These structures include a small bridge, benches, archways, and stairway elements. Originally one of the Arts and Crafts-style influences in America, the Adirondack style forms much of the inspiration for this kind of work. It creates usable sculpture out of bark-covered logs and conveniently shaped tree branches, which can also serve as architectural elements and furniture designs. The rock retaining walls match the facing of the garage at right, which nestles into the same hillside as the main house.

190. Detail showing from the interior the front door of the house in Oakland, California. Graced with an art-glass design adapted from those of the Prairie style, the front door brings light, pattern, and subtle color into the front hall. The translucent glass protects privacy, and the overhang of the upstairs deck acts as a sun break.

191. New house in Oakland, California. A free interpretation of Craftsman-style elements creates a lively sensibility in this hillside house. Familiar forms are used with purpose and vitality, without attempting a period duplication. This is unabashedly contemporary architecture. Forming a foundation to the design is a separate garage at street level (out of view), whose roof, just to the right of the stairs, is used as an open terrace. In the tradition of the Craftsman style, this design celebrates wood, and expresses a variety of textures and joinery details. There is the rhythm of exposed rafter tails under deep eaves, and two prominent chimneys that enliven the gabled roofline. The detailing of the deck railings, with their square cutouts, suggests a Swiss Chalet influence. The palette moves from the color of natural redwood at the base, with blue-gray trim, to mossy gray-green shingles in the upper story. The shingled walls flare out slightly just above the stuccoed level. Partially a basement, the lower level comprises secondary living and utility areas. Up the stairway, recessed below an angled deck area shared by two upper-story bedrooms, is the front porch and main entrance. With a simple shed roof, the porch extends into an open deck area. Overhanging is a private balcony that is outside another bedroom. On the right, the living-room's prow-like projection captures distant views. The house was designed by Rynerson-O'Brien Architecture, with Patrick O'Brien the partner in charge of the project. Winans Construction was the general contractor, and Vasti Porter managed and coordinated the project on behalf of the owners.

192. *(Opposite)* Front hall and staircase of the Oakland house. Light from above dramatizes the staircase balustrade, which incorporates the same square cutout detail used in the exterior railings. More refined in this version, the balustrade is decorated with square ebony pegs set into the cherry posts and balusters, a detail inspired by the work of Greene and Greene. The stair treads are maple, which introduces another wood accent of a lighter color. With a considerable range of color and texture, African slate flooring also blends well with the various colors of wood. The blue-green paint was a popular color in the Arts and Crafts period, and is also used on the ceiling of this area. Anchoring the bottom of the stairs is a square, massive wood-paneled column that conceals built-in storage on its opposite side. The hall leads into the living and dining rooms on the right.

193. Detail of the living-room ceiling of the Oakland house. The all-wood ceiling of the living room angles at one end, where its distinctive window projects. Punctuating the major beam intersections are functional metal fastenings, part of the structural system. There are stained-glass lanterns by Arroyo Craftsman suspended from each of the beams that define the sides of the angled window. Period-style lighting by both the Brass Light Gallery and Rejuvenation Lamp & Fixture Co. was also used on the project.

194. Detail of a window in the family room in the Oakland house. Above a bookcase, one of the built-ins around the fireplace in this room, is this small art-glass window, an adaptation of the Prairie style in glass. The wallpaper frieze has a design of irises and bulrushes by Walter Crane adapted by Bradbury & Bradbury. (The same paper in different colors can be seen in figure 187.) The subdued palette of the art glass and the coloring of the frieze were inspirations for the complex, yet subtle, paint scheme by Edwin Patterson. Besides functioning as an informal living area, this room serves as a media room, and also adjoins a guest bedroom and bath.

195. Detail of the entrance to a house in the San Francisco Bay Area. Complementing the period feeling of the slate roof and copper downspouts, there is an art-glass panel to the left of the front door that was adapted from one by English designer George Walton. A look through the open front door of this new home reveals a second art-glass panel glowing inside. The Tudor-style front door features a knocker and iron strap hinges crafted by Eric Clausen. The design of the house draws on various English Arts and Crafts sources, such as the work of C.F.A. Voysey, as well as that of Charles Rennie Mackintosh and the Glasgow School. Built on a steep hillside, the entrance is on the main living level, which also includes two bedrooms and a staircase that is visible through the front door. Descending the staircase to a lower living area, one reaches a master bedroom, library, and informal living room, all of which open onto a terraced garden area. The house was designed by Rynerson-O'Brien Architecture, with Patrick O'Brien, architect, and Stephen Rynerson, the partner in charge. Crowder Construction was the general contractor.

196. Living room of the house in the San Francisco Bay Area. The striking focal point of the fireplace design, adapted from a work of Charles Rennie Mackintosh, includes built-in shelves that display a collection of African sculpture. The unusual iron grate was forged by Eric Clausen, and there is also a large brass-and-copper fender crafted by Michael Bondi. The room has a coved ceiling with box-beams, in which the central panel is an art-glass skylight that keeps the room evenly lit by day. This photograph was taken from a raised conservatory area, open to the living room, which features copper-lined planting troughs and a dramatic view. On the mantel is a pair of Roycroft candelabra. Partially visible at the extreme left is a tall-case clock by the Shop of the Crafters, and also at the left are a round table, a matching settle, and rocking armchair that are all by Limbert.

197. Master bedroom of the house in the San Francisco Bay Area. The palette of this room was inspired by the soft colors that can be seen in many of the interiors designed by Charles Rennie Mackintosh. The Glasgow Rose is the motif used in the panels of the wallpaper frieze outlined with narrow geometric borders, which was made by Bradbury & Bradbury. The owners designed and embroidered the curtains, adapting motifs originated by designers of the Glasgow School. The design of the bed and nightstands was inspired by a Liberty of London dressing table (out of view), and adapted by Christopher Wright of Berkeley Millworks.

# NOTES

1. *Webster's New Collegiate Dictionary* (Springfield, Mass.: G & C Merriam Co., 1959)

2. *The American Heritage Dictionary of the English Language* (New York: American Heritage Publishing Company and Houghton Mifflin Company, 1969)

3. Paul Atterbury and Clive Wainright, *Pugin: A Gothic Passion* (New Haven, Conn., and London, England: Yale University in association with the Victoria and Albert Museum, 1994), p. 245.

4. Robert Winter, *The California Bungalow* (Los Angeles: Hennessey & Ingalls, Inc., 1980), p. 21.

# A NOTE CONCERNING RESOURCES AND HOW TO LOCATE THEM

There is an ever-increasing range of individual designers, artisans, craftspeople, workshops, manufacturers, antiques dealers, suppliers, and other outlets who are producing or selling furniture, lighting, metalwork, ceramics, glass, textiles, and other decorative objects or accessories in the Arts and Crafts style across the country. Many excellent resources sell their wares nationally by mail order, while others do business on a smaller and more local level.

Although this book does credit a number of fine craftspeople and other Arts and Crafts-related resources whose work appears in the photographs, it is not intended to be perceived as a complete or definitive listing. Also, if the work of a craftsperson or other resource is pictured but not identified, it may be missing because that information was not available or not supplied to us. Considering that possibility, we wish to apologize in advance to anyone whose work may be pictured but who remains uncredited.

As there is not sufficient space in this book to include a definitive list of every noteworthy resource available today, we have instead opted to include a listing of related periodicals, in lieu of a resource guide. Readers will find that many (if not most) of the Arts and Crafts-related resources who sell their wares nationally may be found as regular advertisers in the majority of these periodicals. By consulting them routinely for such information, the likelihood of our readers receiving the most current names, addresses, and telephone numbers for such resources is ensured now and in the future. To find various reputable resources that are specific to individual communities may require a bit of local sleuthing, and it is usually true that personal recommendations and referrals work best in this regard.

## Related Periodicals

*American Bungalow*
123 South Baldwin Avenue,
P.O. Box 756
Sierre Madre, CA 91025-0756
(800) 350-3363

*Style 1900*
17 South Main Street
Lambertville, NJ 08530
(609) 397-4104

*The Craftsman Homeowner*
31 South Grove Street
East Aurora, NY 14052
(716) 652-3333

*Old House Interiors*
2 Main Street
Gloucester, MA 01930
(800) 462-0211

*Old-House Journal*
2 Main Street
Gloucester, MA 01930
(800) 234-3797

*Note:* These periodicals also sell books by mail.

The following is a fine source for books on the Arts and Crafts Movement.

*The Gamble House Bookstore*
4 Westmoreland Place
Pasadena, CA 91003
(818) 449-4178
(Mail order catalog available by request)

For information regarding the Bungalow Heaven Landmark District, please contact:

Bungalow Heaven Neighborhood Association
P.O. Box 40672
Pasadena, CA 91114-7672
(818) 585-2172

# BIBLIOGRAPHY

Adams, Steven. *The Arts and Crafts Movement.* Secaucus, N.J.: Chartwell Books, 1987.

Anderson, Timothy J.; Moore, Eudora M.; Winter, Robert W. (eds.). *California Design 1910.* Pasadena, Calif.: California Design Publications, 1974. Reprint, Santa Barbara, Calif., and Salt Lake City, Utah: Peregrine Smith, Inc., 1980.

Anscombe, Isabelle, and Gere, Charlotte. *Arts and Crafts in Britain and America.* London, England: Academy Editions, 1978.

Aslin, Elizabeth. *The Aesthetic Movement: A Prelude to Art Nouveau.* London, England: Ferndale Editions, 1981.

Atterbury, Paul, and Wainwright, Clive (eds.). *Pugin: A Gothic Passion.* London, England: The Victoria and Albert Museum, 1994.

Bowman, Leslie Greene. *American Arts and Crafts: Virtue in Design.* Los Angeles, Calif.: Los Angeles County Museum of Art, 1990.

Brooks, H. Allen. *Frank Lloyd Wright and the Prairie School.* New York: George Braziller, Inc. in association with Cooper-Hewitt Museum, 1984.

Brown, Henry Collins. *Book of Home Building and Decoration.* New York: Doubleday, Page & Company, 1912.

Clark, Robert Judson (ed.). *The Arts and Crafts Movement in America.* Princeton, N.J.: Princeton University Press, 1972.

Comstock, William Phillips. *Bungalows, Camps and Mountain Houses.* New York: W. T. Comstock Company, 1915 (revised from original edition of 1908). Reprint, Washington, D.C.: The American Institute of Architects Press, 1990.

Cooper, Jeremy. *Victorian and Edwardian Decor.* New York: Abbeville Press, 1987.

Dixon, Walter W., and Tharp, Wayne (eds.). *Dixon's Book of Working Drawings.* Oakland, Calif.: W. W. Dixon Plan Service, (n.d.).

Fermor-Hesketh, Robert. *Architecture of the British Empire.* London, England: George Weidenfeld and Nicholson Ltd., 1986.

Fleming, John; Honour, Hugh; Pevsner, Nikolaus. *The Penguin Dictionary of Architecture.* Harmondsworth, Middlesex, England: Penguin Books Ltd., 1979.

Gebhard, David, and Winter, Robert. *Los Angeles: An Architectural Guide.* Layton, Utah: Gibbs Smith / Peregrine Smith Books, 1994.

Gebhard, David; Sandweiss, Eric; and Winter, Robert. *The Guide to Architecture in San Francisco and Northern California.* Layton, Utah: Gibbs M. Smith, Inc. / Peregrine Smith Books, 1985.

Gordon-Van Tine Company. *117 House Designs of the Twenties.* Davenport, Iowa: Gordon-Van Tine Company, 1923. Reprint, Mineola, N.Y.: The Atheneum of Philadelphia and Dover Publications, Inc., 1992.

Gowans, Alan. *The Comfortable House: North American Suburban Architecture 1890–1930.* Cambridge, Mass.: MIT Press, 1989.

Gray, Stephen (ed.). *The Mission Furniture of L. & J. G. Stickley.* New York: Turn of the Century Editions, 1983. (Material is reprinted from various catalogs.)

Grow, Lawrence. *The Old House Book of Cottages and Bungalows.* Pittstown, N.J.: The Main Street Press, Inc., 1987.

Harding, James. *The Pre-Raphaelites.* New York: Rizzoli International Publications, Inc., 1977.

Jones, Robert T. (ed.). *Authentic Small Houses of the Twenties.* New York: Harper and Brothers Publishers, 1929. Reprint, New York: Dover Publications, Inc., 1987.

Kaplan, Wendy, *"The Art That Is Life": The Arts and Crafts Movement in America, 1875–1920.* Boston, Mass.: Little, Brown and Company, 1987.

Lancaster, Clay. *The American Bungalow.* New York: Abbeville Press, 1985.

Loizeaux, J. D. *Classic Houses of the Twenties.* Elizabeth, N.J.: J. D. Loizeaux Lumber Company and the Loizeaux Builders Supply Co., 1927. Reprint, Mineola, N.Y.: The Atheneum of Philadelphia and Dover Publications, Inc., 1992.

Makinson, Randell L. *Greene and Greene: Architecture as Fine Art*. Salt Lake City, Utah: Gibbs M. Smith Inc. / Peregrine Smith Books, 1977.

_____ . *Greene and Greene: Furniture and Related Designs*. Salt Lake City, Utah: Gibbs M. Smith, Inc. / Peregrine Smith Books, 1979.

McAlester, Virginia and Lee. *A Field Guide to American Houses*. New York: Alfred A. Knopf, Inc., 1984.

McCoy, Esther. *Five California Architects*. New York: Praeger Publishers, Inc., 1960.

Morgan Woodwork Organization. *Building with Assurance*. Oshkosh, Wis.: Morgan Woodwork Organization, 1921.

Morrison, Hugh. *Louis Sullivan: Prophet of Modern Architecture*. New York: W. W. Norton Company, 1935.

Saylor, Henry H. *Bungalows*. New York: Robert M. McBride and Co., 1911.

Sears, Roebuck and Company. *Sears, Roebuck Catalog of Houses, 1926*. Chicago, Ill., and Philadelphia, Pa.: Sears, Roebuck and Company, 1926. Reprint, New York: The Atheneum of Philadelphia and Dover Publications, Inc., 1991.

Sherwin-Williams Company Decorative Department. *Your Home and Its Decoration*. (n.p.): The Sherwin-Williams Company, 1910.

Stickley, Gustav. *The Best of Craftsman Homes*. Santa Barbara, Calif., and Salt Lake City, Utah: Peregrine Smith, Inc., 1979. (Includes plans from Stickley's *Craftsman Homes* (1909) and *More Craftsman Homes* (1912).

_____ . *Craftsman Bungalows: 59 Homes from "The Craftsman."* Mineola, N.Y.: Dover Publications, Inc., 1988. (This book reprints thirty-six articles selected from issues of *The Craftsman* magazine published between December 1903 and August 1916.)

Trapp, Kenneth R. (ed.). *The Arts and Crafts Movement in California: Living the Good Life*. New York: Abbeville Press Publishers, 1993.

Van Rensselaer, Mariana Griswold. *Henry Hobson Richardson and His Works*. New York: Houghton, Mifflin and Company, 1888. Reprint, New York: Dover Publications, Inc., 1969.

Via, Maria, and Searle, Marjorie (eds.) *Head, Heart and Hand: Elbert Hubbard and the Roycrofters*. Rochester, New York: University of Rochester Press, 1994.

Watkinson, Ray. *William Morris as Designer*. London, England: Cassell Ltd., 1967.

Wilson, Henry L. *California Bungalows of the Twenties*. Los Angeles, Calif.: Henry L. Wilson, (n.d.). Reprint, Mineola, N.Y.: Dover Publications, Inc., 1993.

Winter, Robert. *The California Bungalow*. Los Angeles, Calif.: Hennessey & Ingalls, Inc., 1980.

Woodbridge, Sally (ed.). *Bay Area Houses: New Edition*. Layton, Utah: Gibbs M. Smith Inc., 1988.

# NOTES BY THE PHOTOGRAPHER

I grew up in a house that could easily be described as a legacy of the bungalow. If you drive by 724 South 45th Street in Lincoln, Nebraska, you'll see a little cracker box of a house. Hastily constructed in the postwar (that's World War II) building boom, it has all of the charm of a bowl of oatmeal. You see, by then all of the charm and rusticity that had existed in conventional housing had fallen by the wayside. Gone were the exposed wood ceilings, pergolas, sweeping porches, handmade lighting fixtures, and clinker brick. They were replaced with sheetrock, formica, wall-to-wall carpet (well, at least in our house, since my father was a carpet salesman for Gold & Co.), and chrome-plated everything. What remained, however, was the bungalow's amazing floor plan. Tiny spaces flowed together making them seem larger. An ample screened back porch opened to a large yard and garden. And a narrow enclosed stairway led to an attic that was later developed into a child's bedroom—mine, to be exact. Like most houses in Nebraska, ours possessed a basement. Here we found welcome coolness during the hot steamy days of summer, and in the winter we played endless games while the persistent chilling winds howled outside.

When we went on short trips it was usually to see some nearby relative. These were all folks with an agrarian background, and they lived in towns like Friend and Fairbury. They all lived in bungalows. Real bungalows built at the turn of the century. The kind that are in this book. Sturdy little buildings built with real materials that still stand today. Thus, when the prospect of photographing this book came up it seemed like a return to my youth.

Now to the nuts and bolts of photographing these little jewels. Paul and I scouted out the houses and shot 35mm snapshots. We than made our selections and went back to take the "real" photograph. For the final photograph I shot on Fuji Provia™ transparency film (exceptional whites, consistent color although a little troublesome in deep shade). I shot on a 4x5 Sinar F™ with a full complement of lenses from 65mm to 180mm. One of the predominant features of bungalows is that they have large overhanging porch roofs. While the vision of sitting on a porch swing on a bright sunny day may be pleasing to the mind and the eye it is not pleasing to the eye of a camera. If the photographer exposes for the porch, the rest of the house gets blasted out with light. If one exposes for the house, the porch goes black. With that in mind when photographing the exteriors, we tried to pick overcast days when the light was more even. Other times we shot late in the day when

*Photo by Lance Lougee*

the sun was streaming into the porch. A number of bungalows were shot in the evening, letting the interior light evoke the spirit of hearth and home.

Shooting the interiors posed a different set of challenges. The spaces can be small and are frequently quite dark. The wood surfaces seem to suck up all of the light while inviting reflections from any direct supplemental lighting. Using a hand viewfinder Paul and I selected the angle for shooting the room. While Paul busied himself with styling the room I worked on the lighting. Usually I used a Novatron 1600™ with a Whitedome™ for a main light. The Novatron flash units have a lot of "bang for the buck," and I highly recommend them. The Whitedome™, manufactured by Photoflex is similar to most softboxes except light comes out from all sides instead of just from the front. Kind of like a large, very soft, bare tube head. Other lights powered by Novatron power packs were placed throughout the room. I then calculated my exposure by blending ambient light with light from the flashes. We checked the results with Polaroids before exposing the final film.

All film was processed normally using the services of Fisher Photo in Emeryville, California, Custom Process in Berkeley, California, and Consolidated Media Services (CMS) in Pasadena, California. Hats off to the folks at CMS—open until 11:00PM during the week and 6:00PM on Saturday—a working photographer's dream. Thanks also to Bill and Dr. Bob. Keep comin' back.

DOUGLAS KEISTER